The Pune Diaries

a love affair with India

The Pune Diaries

a love affair with India

Anand Subhuti

CINNAMONTEAL
PUBLISHING

First published in India in 2014 by CinnamonTeal Publishing

Copyright © 2014 Anand Subhuti

ISBN 978–93–84129–46–0

Author's website: www.anandsubhuti.com

Typesetting and Cover Design: CinnamonTeal Publishing

Page embellishments: Robot/vectorstock

The photographic image on page 27 is used under license, with permission from the copyright holder: Dinodia Photo Library, Mumbai.

The artistic sketches on page 13 and page 138 are drawn by Savita Korte.

The painting of Osho Auditorium on page 177 is by Meera Hashimoto.

CinnamonTeal Publishing,
Plot No 16, Housing Board Colony
Gogol, Margao
Goa 403601 India
www.cinnamonteal.in

Introduction

If I stay away from India too long – say, more than six months – I begin to miss it. I start longing for that feeling of being surrounded by India's sounds, smells, colours and chaos. I want to be immersed in it all once more.

But if I remain in India too long – say, more than four months – I feel an increasingly desperate need to escape. I wait impatiently for that moment when my plane takes off and heads towards those clean, cool, carefully manicured countries in Northern Europe.

This is my relationship with India. It's a love affair that demands lots of togetherness, but also requires a good deal of space between visits. It's a push-pull, yes-no, love-hate kind of thing. Most probably, by the time you've finished reading this little book, you'll understand why.

This is a personal journal of my most recent visit, written between my arrival on November 28, 2013, and my departure on March 22, 2014. The diary entries have no dates, but are presented in chronological sequence, spanning the time frame.

Mostly, I talk about my life in Pune, a city I've been visiting for years. The journal also includes a trip to the beaches of Goa, but I have decided to keep the title as 'Pune Diaries' because this was the main focus for me. Besides, even in the entries about the beach, most of the people involved with me are somehow connected to Pune.

And now, the journey begins...

Pune Diary 1

Up the Ghats

It makes for a sleepless night, that's for sure, but I like to arrive at Mumbai Airport after midnight – courtesy of Jet Airways from Heathrow – because in these early hours of the morning the great city sleeps. You can cruise quickly through empty streets instead of fighting through endless daytime traffic jams.

That is, of course, if your taxi wallah is on time and waiting as you emerge from the arrivals lounge – my eyes travel along a row of 50-or-more Indian men holding notices with people's names – and yes, there he is, same guy as last time. We exchange a friendly handshake, then he takes over my baggage trolley and off we go to the nearby parking zone.

Even though it's the tail end of November and the monsoon is long gone, the night air is warm, humid and sticky – must be the closeness of the ocean. It also has that recycled feeling, as if it's already been breathed by a million souls.

In spite of empty streets it seems to take forever to leave the metropolis, skirting slum colonies, negotiating half-constructed flyovers and passing massive apartment blocks that probably contain the same number of people that populated this entire country a couple of hundred years ago. I should be laying down my weary head on the back seat to sleep, but I have to look, soaking it all up, as if reminding myself that, yes, once again, I am in India.

"Taxi business good?" I ask Sattar, my driver, trying to open up a conversation.

Without taking his eyes off the road, he shakes his head.

"Business no good."

"Many people coming to Pune?"

"People not coming."

Hmm. Seems like a conversational cul de sac. I switch to another topic.

"Heavy monsoon this year? Much rain?"

"No raining now."

"No, I mean... during the monsoon... much rain?"

"Monsoon over... dry season now... "

And that's about it for chit-chat. Sattar and I have known each other seemingly forever, since I always book the same taxi. But he has little English and me, alas, no Hindi – disgraceful after 38 years in this country.

Eventually, we leave the suburbs and now we're on the six-lane Mumbai-Pune Expressway, picking up speed and racing headlong into the night. Soon, the road begins its climb up the Western Ghats, a mountain range that runs for a thousand miles along the Western side of India, separating the coastal plain from the Deccan Plateau.

Here, a strange mutation occurs. Expressway lanes that were completely empty a few minutes ago, while driving on the flat, are suddenly crowded with trucks as we hit the hill. Sattar weaves expertly through convoys of slow-moving lorries, their engines roaring and exhaust pipes belching smoke as they strain to make the grade.

Ahead of us, a heavily-laden behemoth is inching its way up the crawler lane and things get problematic for us when another truck, barely moving faster, pulls out to overtake –

effectively blocking two lanes for the next half-hour – while the so-called 'fast lane' seems permanently occupied by a passenger coach matching our speed.

But Sattar is not to be thwarted. He swings the taxi onto the shoulder, taking the behemoth on the inside, then veers out to the fast lane ahead of the coach, then back on the shoulder... slipping like a cunning fox through a herd of motorized elephants.

I love this part of the journey. It's awesome driving, like nowhere else on earth and everyone knows that if even one truck breaks down on the hill the whole procession will stagger to a halt.

Back in the 70s, when this highway was a narrow,

winding, badly-paved road, naked sadhus wearing only holy markings on their foreheads used to sit at the foot of the ghats and stare with unforgiving eyes at the truck drivers as they began the climb. Their unspoken message: "Buddy, if you have any hope at all of making it, you'd better throw me some coins... "

Most drivers did, or rather, their assistants did, because there were never less than three men in any truck cab. Their most crucial job, in the event of a breakdown, was to leap out and jam big rocks behind the wheels to prevent a roll back.

Tonight we're lucky... up, up, up we go... ... through the tunnel at the top... up a little more and then, yes, we're on the plateau. We've already passed the vacation town of Lonavla and a few minutes later it's time to pull into a wayside truck stop for a chai break.

Chai is the Indian working man's espresso: a tiny cup of super-sweet, super-strong, spicy black tea. It's normally served twice a day, at mid-morning and around 4:30 in the afternoon, but here on the highway it's consumed 24/7 by drivers needing to stay awake.

Ten minutes later, we're back on the road, which, obeying the same mysterious law of traffic migration, is again free of trucks. Where do they go?

We drive into Pune well before dawn, travelling swiftly through more empty streets and soon I recognize the landmarks – a bridge, a temple, a government building, the back of the railway station – and smile in the knowledge that our destination, Koregaon Park, is just a couple of minutes away.

Where to stay? This year I'm determined NOT to have to deal with the traffic on North Main Road, which in recent times has become totally insane. So my old room in Rag Vilas Society, down by the river, is out of the question, because it's on the wrong side of the tracks. I've got to find a room *inside* Koregaon Park, close to the meditation resort.

I tell the driver to head for Hotel Sunderban, whose only real virtue as a guest house is that it's located literally next door to the resort. It has super-expensive rooms, well out of my price range, but also cheap ones for casual, drop-in clientele, which you cannot book ahead of time. First come, first served.

The taxi pulls in and I slowly clamber out, walking stiffly after the three-hour drive, and have to wake up the concierge, who, quite naturally, is sleeping at his desk.

"Good morning. You have a cheap room for me?" I inquire hopefully.

He nods, groping under the desk for a key with one hand and opening the register with the other. He's done this so many times he could do it in his sleep, which is probably just as well – I don't think he's actually awake.

"Number nine... passport please... "

I'm in luck. One of Sunderban's cheapest rooms is vacant. It means shared showers and toilets, which is not much fun, and the ones downstairs are unspeakably dirty, but the upstairs bathroom is shiny and new. It's just a little irritating when the staff pass through and say "good morning sir" when I'm cleaning my teeth.

The hotel is so close to the resort that I won't need to rent a locker and there's tea in bed in the morning – thank god for room service. Now, let's try and get a few hours' sleep.

Pune Diary 2

Planet Osho

This moment always seems surreal: walking into the meditation resort's 'welcome centre' for the first time around mid-morning after a long trip and little sleep. The place is super-quiet, in mind-blowing contrast to the noisy streets outside. The black marble décor makes it dark and cool and you look out on this little garden, with green groundcover spreading over small rolling hillocks.

A rippling stream with big red fish winds through these 'hills' and a white marble Buddha sits in detached splendour above it all. Tall trees overhang the area, adding more shade, and beyond the garden a few distant figures, wearing maroon robes, glide unhurriedly along pathways in front of black buildings.

When you're jet lagged and disoriented like I am now, it seems like entering another world, which, come to think of it, is exactly what it is. This isn't India or the West. It's somewhere else entirely... Planet Osho.

When I first came here, in 1976, the place was crowded with young, hairy, Western adventurers in love with the spiritual mysteries of the East. We wore bright orange clothes – the traditional colour of *sannyas* in India – and necklaces of wooden beads with Osho's photo dangling from it in a locket. We spent most of our time hugging, meditating, dancing, singing and sleeping with each other.

To outsiders, we must've looked like a bunch of sexualized hippies, searching for the ultimate orgasm, which, if you define meditation as 'orgasm without sex' – as Osho once did – is pretty close to the truth. The place has changed. So have I.

The staff in the welcome centre work quietly. Most are new to me, but one or two know me and we smile in recognition. I cruise through the mandatory AIDS test, pick up my credit card-sized pass, buy a day sticker and then head over to the 'Galleria', the resort's clothing shop, to buy a new maroon robe and a pair of maroon pants.

There's no doubt about it, the colour of maroon, in all its modest range of shades, is eternally in fashion here in the world of Osho.

But I'm not staying, just registering. There's other, more important, arrival stuff for me to take care of first. Exiting the resort, I catch a rickshaw from the main gate to nearby German Bakery Lane and guide the driver to the end of the street, then turn left and arrive outside a small shop called Gulshan Forex where a neatly-dressed, chain-smoking gentleman called Shankar changes money.

He also stores trunks in his loft and that's why I'm here. Mine have been lying in the loft for eight months, ever since my departure last April. I know the drill: first, I need to hire two, strong-looking rickshaw wallahs from the nearby taxi line and then, with their help, Shankar drags a couple of big, silver-coloured metal trunks to the trapdoor in the ceiling and slides them slowly down the ladder.

With much heaving, staggering and complaining – "too much heavy sir", which translates as "you will need to pay us more" – the drivers carry the trunks out to the waiting rickshaws and somehow jam one into each passenger compartment.

14

If you've never seen a rickshaw, they are strange creatures, rather like a motorbike with a double-wide passenger seat behind the driver and the whole thing covered with a large yellow plastic hood. They have two-stroke, petrol-and-oil burning engines and are a wonderful source of atmospheric pollution.

Since both back seats are buried beneath my trunks, I share a driver's seat up front, sitting with half my butt dangling in empty space, my hands clinging to the sides of the cab, as we begin the short but uncomfortable journey back to my hotel.

Outside the entrance, the staff boys take over and carry the trunks to my room. I pay off the drivers – 100 rupees each keeps them satisfied – tip the bell boys, then close the door and search through my backpack for a tiny bunch of keys to unlock the trunks.

And, yes… here they are… and, yes… the keys work! I pat myself on the back. It's simply amazing that I haven't lost this little bunch of keys during the eight months I've been away in Europe, travelling between the UK, Denmark and Russia.

I peer inside a trunk, pull out some maroon robes and sniff cautiously. Not bad. The smell of monsoon mould is detectable, absorbed during the long weeks and months of India's wet season, but the odour isn't too strong and there are no mould marks.

Nevertheless, everything has to go to the dhobi for washing and that's why I always buy a new maroon outfit in the resort's Galleria each year on arrival: to tide me over while the annual washing rituals are observed.

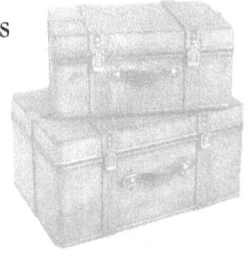

Pune Diary 3

Not for the faint-hearted

"German Bakery Lane, please."

"Yes, baba."

The rickshaw driver reaches down with his left hand to grasp a lever close to the floor and yanks it upward. Nothing. Two more tries and his efforts are rewarded. The little two-stroke engine coughs into life. He pulls the steering bar hard to the left and noses out into the traffic, making a 180-degree turn, and races away from the resort's main gate, heading for North Main Road.

And now, stand by for a local traffic hazard announcement: there is a new 'fear meditation' available for sannyasins wishing to travel via rickshaw from the Osho Resort to nearby German Bakery Lane, as I am now doing. It goes like this:

Until recently, one could drive from the resort's front gate to North Main Road, turn left and join the flow of traffic for a short distance and then turn right into German Bakery Lane.

Left... right... into GB Lane you go... a short, easy trip with no serious challenges.

However, in a bid to speed up the traffic, that section of North Main Road has been turned into a dual carriageway, making it impossible to turn into GB Lane from our side of the street.

So, if you're in a rickshaw, coming from the ashram front gate, your driver now reaches the junction with North Main

Road and, instead of turning left, he makes use of a small gap in the central divider to cross the busy carriageway to the other side and then drives AGAINST the traffic flow until he can turn into GB Lane.

One of Osho's favourite pieces of spiritual guidance to his disciples was 'go with the flow', but here we struggle against it. Of course, this is crazy. We should go all the way to the main highway, make a U-turn and come back, but rickshaw wallahs have a unique sense of priorities. They don't mind facing an on-rushing horde of motorbikes and cars, all blasting their horns, if they can shorten a local trip by a few hundred metres.

This is not a meditation for the faint-hearted, nor for tender souls emerging from the resort's therapy courses in delicate, sensitive spaces. But if you feel like screaming in terror there's nothing quite like it.

Now, about my washing: I could have used the hotel's laundry service but with so much stuff I figure it's cheaper to take it all to the dhobi in GB Lane, whose bizarre emporium is located at the end of a short side-alley. You can't miss it. It's the one that looks like it got bombed along with the bakery in 2010. How this man manages to make clothes clean in this chaotic jumble is a miracle... you can't even figure out if his place has walls and a roof.

He counts it all methodically, sorting my dirty belongings into piles: one for maroon clothes used as daytime wear in the resort, one for white robes used only at night for the 'Evening Meeting', one for ordinary street clothes, one for towels and sheets. "Tomorrow evening," he assures me.

Back in the rickshaw we head for a small shop run by Arti, a little old lady who sells just about everything a sannyasin needs: robes, dresses, pants, bed sheets, bed covers, meditation chairs, pillows...

But this year it's different: I'm selling, not buying. You see, I've come to a momentous decision: I'm downsizing, throwing away most of my storage stuff; saying, in effect, that the days of making a home for myself in Pune are over.

I pull up outside Arti's shop with one of my big trunks crammed with belongings and, with a little help from the rickshaw driver, carry it over to her emporium.

She is not surprised. "Everyone now is same," she says, "One trunk only! Nobody wants to keep things anymore." That's true. Back in the 80s and 90s, people furnished and maintained whole houses in the Koregaon Park area, because they stayed year-round, or at least 6-9 months. Then, after Osho died, the community that had gathered around him slowly broke up and everybody adjusted to the new paradigm: short visits in winter and minimum storage for the following year.

Arti looks at my treasure trove. "I give you one thousand," she says, which is way too little for all these quilts and sheets and blankets, not to mention my space heater and the trunk itself, but hey, a single lady has to make a living somehow. Arti's husband, who used to sit outside her shop all day while she ran the business, passed away some years back.

"Okay," I nod in agreement and the deal is done. Wheeee! A great feeling of unburdening and relief. Now just one light trunk remains – and one lighter swami, too.

Pune Diary 4

Spiritual diseases

Arrival in Pune would not be complete without a sore throat, cough and irritated sinuses. Yes, the potent local cocktail of polluted air and germs got to me fast this time. It's a familiar bug that I've had before, a swiftly moving virus with three stops: starts in the throat, goes up into the nose, then down into the lungs. It seems like this year I have a mild attack so the worst should be over in 2-3 days, although the cough is sure to last longer.

Meanwhile, it's time to lie back on my hotel bed, watch feel-good movies on my laptop and surround myself with my old friends: a bottle of cough syrup, a pack of brightly-coloured blue ayurvedic pills, eucalyptus oil for steam inhalations, and truckloads of paracetamol and vitamin C.

One tablet is missing from my usual collection: a popular ayurvedic cold cure that tastes terrible and seems effective but which, so recent internet rumour has it, contains unacceptable levels of mercury, lead and arsenic.

"Watch out! 600 times the safety limit!" warns a friend from France. It's probably a scare story he read on Facebook but still, I think I'll skip it this time. Pity, though, it worked well; the taste was so horrible you had to get well.

The immediate effect of my sickness is, of course, to slow everything down, so that, having arrived here at Western speed, I cannot maintain momentum. Instead,

I'm confined to bed with sneezing fits, coughing attacks and generally feeling like a lost soul who's stumbled into a swamp and is now slowly being sucked under. Thank god

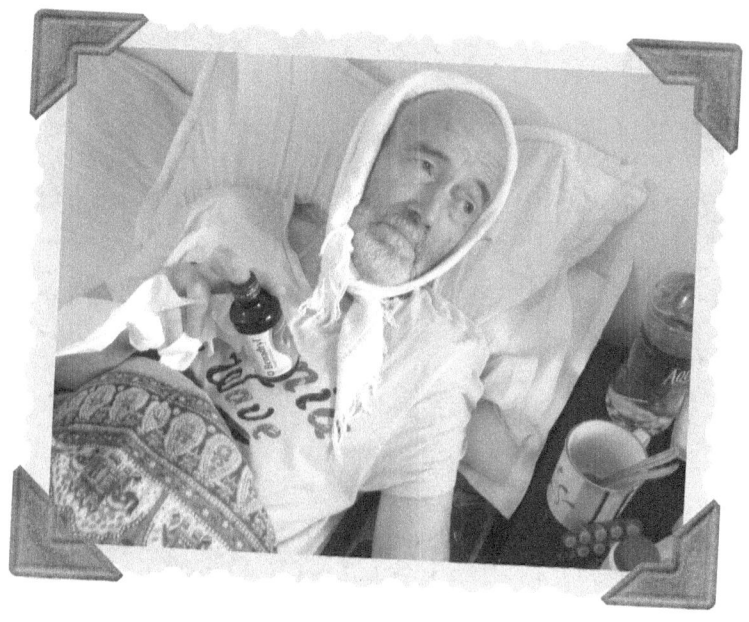

for friends with 30 GB memory sticks loaded with pirated movies and a laptop on which to watch them.

In India, sickness has its meditative side. Back in the 70s, we used to call Hepatitis A 'the spiritual disease' because although it seemed accidental when you got it – usually from contaminated water or fresh-squeezed juices – it was usually well-timed, just when you needed a compulsory meditation retreat.

'Hep' was an invitation to experience the miracle of non-doing, because for six weeks you were too weak to move a muscle, to do anything at all. A journey to the bathroom was a huge project, so there was really nothing to do except lie on your bed, be admired by your friends for looking romantically yellow – oh those deep, soulful, mustard-coloured eyes! – and watch geckos catching flies on the ceiling, which they tended to do, as I recall, about once an hour.

Some people's minds slowed down so much they thought they'd attained spiritual enlightenment.

"I knew it would happen one day, I just didn't know it would be today," pronounced one yellow seeker, gazing with the serene certainty of self-realization into his girlfriend's eyes. She worked in Osho's house and passed on the conversation to the mystic himself, who sent the message back:

"Keep meditating and watch the ego."

Hi-tech filtration systems and bottled water have made hepatitis a rarity for tourists these days, but a shot of local flu, nicely laced with polluted air, will definitely slow things down for a while. The cold weather doesn't help, because it keeps smoky air trapped near the ground and the night watchmen guarding Koregaon Park's mansions and apartment buildings will burn anything – rubber tires and plastic bags included – to keep warm in the early hours.

By the way, for the uninitiated and unprepared, there are three things that people tend to forget when visiting India:

1) How cold it gets in winter (Dec/Jan).
2) How hot it gets in summer (April/May).
3) How wet it gets in the monsoon (July/August/Sept).

Now the temperature is down to nine degrees at night and I ask for extra blankets from the hotel staff to transform my room into a cosy sick ward. Room service brings me tea and toast. Cate Blanchette is giving an excellent performance in *Blue Jasmine* on my laptop screen and nobody expects me to do anything.

Ah India... It's good to be here once more.

Pune Diary 5

Open to the sky

The white marble floor of Buddha Grove has been polished like never before, so it looks as smooth as glass. In fact, when the sun shines, it looks wet, as if covered with a layer of sparkling clear water. Amazing! This big, oval-shaped open space is shimmering like a mirage in a desert.

Of course, it's going to be a real challenge to keep the 'Grove so pristine. Every morning, 50-100 visitors gather here to dance freestyle to music ranging from pop to profound, depending on the *DJ du jour*. So many feet scuffing the surface... so many leaves falling from the surrounding trees... so many birds sitting on branches above, doing what comes naturally. Unless cleaning is continuous the shiny surface soon dulls and disappears beneath layers of dirt.

One of the driving forces behind the marble polishing marathon is Bodhi Hannah, an 84 year-old German sannyasin who comes here every evening with her enormous Japanese bow to shoot arrows at distant targets. She loves the noble art of Zen archery and sometimes I watch her, noticing how she goes through the elaborate ritual: bowing down to the target before shooting... fitting the arrow to the string... raising the great bow above her head and then bringing it down and aiming all in one smooth movement.

The thing is, if you watch her and don't look at the target, you simply can't tell if she's scored a bull's eye or missed the target altogether. Her slow, graceful movements are the same, her facial expression is the same. I like that. In Zen, it's the process, not the result that matters.

Anyway, Bodhi Hannah can also be seen, on many mornings, carefully cleaning stains which the staff's big industrial scrubbing machines haven't been able to wash from the marble.

"I have to keep after them, ja?" she grumbles philosophically, stepping back to check the results of her labour. "They do okay, but they also miss a lot."

Flashback: for much of its 35 year-old existence, this floor was protected from natural elements. It was built in the late 70s and christened 'Buddha Hall', a meditation space where Osho arrived every morning at 8:00 am to give his daily discourse. It had a simple roof of corrugated metal sheets, supported by wooden posts – all covered with white cloth to make it look nice.

But Osho didn't like poles. He liked to see everybody. So, in the late 80s, when the mystic returned to Pune after his years in Oregon and his World Tour, his sannyasins created a huge steel arch, right across the hall, and draped a massive plastic canopy over the top, rather like a big tent. The open sides were surrounded by a much-proclaimed 'world's largest mosquito net' – it never made the Guinness Book of Records, though.

The tent structure lasted until 2002 when a new construction, Osho Auditorium, opened its doors for the first time. Rumour has it that, by then, the steel arch was way beyond its 'use by' safety date, being constructed of massive steel boxes that were welded together and then held in place by steel ropes.

However, as I recall, it wasn't so much the decaying arch that drove us out of there, but the steadily mounting indignation of the neighbours – those poor, long-suffering local home owners who'd been putting up with our loud music and noisy 'active meditation' techniques since 1974.

The legendary Indian character trait of spiritual tolerance had finally worn thin and they were on the verge of launching a campaign to shut us down when the new, fully-enclosed, sound-proof Osho Auditorium took much of our noise inside.

Oh yes, and during its whole career, Buddha Hall never had planning permission. Osho wasn't big on 'asking' before 'doing' and anyway the Pune Corporation hated us so much they would never have given us their blessings.

Okay, enough of nostalgia. Now, all roofs have gone and this open-to-the-sky, rechristened 'Buddha Grove' hosts one of my favourite activities: the morning dance celebration, when, during an hour of music – with decibel levels carefully monitored – people in maroon robes come and dance in the sunshine, any way they like. It's a time to move the body, greet friends, gossip, flirt a little and get lost in the dance.

Some people wear shoes, some love to be barefoot. Let's hope we don't leave too many marks for Bodhi Hannah to clean up.

Pune Diary 6

Holding on, letting go

"Here they come."

"Where?"

There... to the side of the pyramid... flying low... three of them."

"Right... and here come two more... and two more... "

As usual, I arrive early outside Osho Auditorium for the Evening Meeting. It's a nice moment of waiting and relaxation: standing with other white-robed meditators, close to the little artificial lake that separates us from the big, black auditorium. When it was being designed, Osho said he wanted people to cross a bridge over water to get to the meditation space... symbolism for the seeker leaving the world behind.

My Swedish friend, Aphrodite, likes to come early, too, so together we enjoy the fading light and watch the big fruit bats fly over our heads at tree-top level, their dark, prehistoric shapes silhouetted against the slowly dimming light of the Western sky.

They look menacing, scary, especially in the form of black silhouettes, as they pass silently overhead, as if they could suddenly dive down and bite your neck, like a vampire bat from hell. But in reality they're harmless, eating only fruit.

The bats do their fly-by routine every evening, heralding our time to meditate. They live in a grove of old trees on the other side of Pune, by the river, and every evening fly across the city to their feeding stations in Koregaon Park and beyond.

Apparently, these bats are called 'flying dogs' in some countries and 'flying foxes' in others. I saw one up close last year. He grabbed hold of a power line with his claw-like feet, which would've been okay except when he was hanging downwards his nose touched another power line below it. An electrifying experience!

Poor guy. He fell to earth, enabling me to see his features: two big front teeth like a rat, face like a small dog, ears like a fox, brown fur body of a squirrel, but no tail – just long, black, shiny, pterodactyl-style wings straight out of Jurassic Park.

These guys live off fruit from the giant banyan and baobab trees around Koregaon Park and you certainly know when it's happening because the ground beneath the tree is covered with a circular, brown carpet of half-chewed fruit. Bats eat this stuff, but humans don't, as far as I know.

Anyway, I also notice, inside the resort, that whenever a tree is in fruit and the ground is littered with debris, the walls of the black buildings surrounding the tree get covered in brown streaks of an unknown substance – well, not really unknown, because, of course, it's bat shit.

Bats don't go to the bathroom when they're hanging upside down -- naturally, because they would cover themselves with their own emissions. Not very nice for a well-groomed bat. So... what happens?

It seems they have a super-fast digestion rate. They find a tree-full of fruit and then stuff themselves all night long, while hanging upside down on the branches. Then, at a certain moment, when they've eaten enough, they let go of the branch and fall towards the ground. Opening their wings and starting to flap, they pull out of the dive and zoom upwards, releasing a fast-moving stream of digested fruit products as they do so.

Technical aviation detail: they probably use the point of maximum g-force, which pilots know when they pull out of a plane dive, as a convenient release mechanism for their digestion.

Within the confined space of the resort, with almost no distance between a tree and a building, there can only be one result: dozens of brown streaks on shiny black walls and one long cleaning job for the staff. Thank you for sharing guys.

I don't see much of a parallel between bats and sannyasins, but we are both challenged by the dynamic between two opposing forces: holding on and letting go. Bats hold onto branches and stuff themselves until they have to let go. As sannyasins, we hold on to our worldly attachments until someone like Osho comes along and invites us to let go and fall into nothingness. Personally, I think bats have it easier.

Pune Diary 7

Carry me home...

Carry me home... to the wonderland
Where my heart can shine...
Carry me home... to the wonderland
Inside...

I love singing this song, which was played last night by a live band at Celebrating Sannyas, now held in the resort's Plaza area. This is the time when people who want to commit to the spiritual path have their new name announced over the sound system. They come forward, out of the crowd, and sit on black zafu cushions in an open space, under an all-glass pyramid roof, listening to a quote from Osho that guides them inwards.

After the quote, the band plays a slow meditative number for a few minutes, then shifts gear to a fast dance rhythm. At this point, the seated ones stand up and their friends rush in from the sides and hug them, then we all dance together.

I don't know whose idea it was to shift the event from Osho Auditorium to the Plaza but it's a definite improvement. The whole thing has a friendlier feeling to it. Maybe it's because of the open-air cappuccino bar behind us and the easy flow of people between the ceremony and the café.

Maybe, too, it's because the Plaza pyramid is lit up at night and looks spectacular - all black marble and tinted glass – like a fusion of the Hard Rock Café and an ancient temple in Atlantis.

It's hard to say, in a few words – or even with a lot of words – what 'celebrating sannyas' really means. I guess it refers to some kind of realisation, which comes upon a few of us, that there's more to life than a job, a career, or raising a family. In short, there's more to life than the external world offers.

That's why Osho talks so much about 'going in'. Basically, he's encouraging people to begin a journey of self-exploration, or self-inquiry, to discover the nature of one's personal consciousness.

'Sannyas' is an ancient tradition in India, passed on by god-knows-how-many gurus, sadhus, yogis and mahatmas, but if you decide to take sannyas in Pune it's probably because you feel some kind of rapport with Osho – even though he died 24 years ago.

Here, the whole event is carried on the wings of music, which creates the ambience and atmosphere needed to give significance to this simple ceremony. No music, no celebration – it's that simple.

I usually get a sneak preview of the songs. The band rehearses all morning in a small room behind the Galleria. You can hear them on your way to lunch in Meera Canteen and peek in the window to see who's in the line-up. The talent is in-depth and the music usually succeeds in bridging the considerable gap between rock 'n roll and meditation.

For me, the really impressive thing is that it all hangs on whether there are enough musicians and singers around to make up a band. People are coming and going from the resort all the time, so it's never the same line-up for two weeks running.

Arjun, French-Canadian guitarist and all-round musician, heads up the band and it's fascinating to watch him conduct it, live, during the celebration. It's almost like they wing it, shifting from guitar riffs to drum solos to acapella singing, making it up as they go along.

I guess it's always been a dream of mine to sing in a band, but so far I didn't get further than a humorous song in one of the resort's *Meditators Got Talent* variety shows. With a couple of friends, I sang a remix of Bob Marley's *No Woman, No Cry*, adapting the lyrics to be more culturally relevant for India, singing *No Sugar, No Chai*.

Meanwhile, the Pune winter weather is weird and

unpredictable. The cold evenings disappeared for a few nights but now they're back again, so I found myself in the embarrassing situation of having to revisit Arti, the little old lady with the all-purpose shop at the end of German Bakery Lane, and asking her "Can I have the blanket you bought from me a week ago? It's too cold at night!"

She gave it to me without charge. "Just bring it back to me when you leave," she said.

Bless her.

Pune Diary 8

Sounds of Koregaon park

My stay in Pune has been transformed, thanks to a lucky break. My dear friend, Sucheta, decided to go back to Stockholm to take care of a chronic shoulder problem, so I was able to move into her room in a house behind the resort. No more hotel shared bathrooms and no crossing North Main Road!

Here, I am in sannyasin paradise, sitting in my new room on a Sunday afternoon, with the door to the balcony open, a gentle breeze rustling the bamboo leaves outside and sunshine bathing the nearby trees.

The sounds are so familiar: shrieks of fast-flying green parakeets as they zoom past the house, lazy cawing of well-fed crows and the chirping of many other birds calling to each other among the branches. There are frequent train whistles – a sound that goes back in my memory more than 30 years as Pune continues its function as one of India's main railway junctions.

The tracks are less than half-a-mile away from Koregaon Park. Steam whistles have been replaced by electric horns but the effect is remarkably similar, especially when they sound off together, in twos and threes, like the opening notes of a yet-to-be-composed symphony.

My peace is temporarily disturbed by the noisy buzzing of a rickshaw as it races along South Main Road, but otherwise there's very little traffic. I notice the sound of distant Hindi devotional singing, definitely a recording, with those typical high-pitched female voices that make me think of colourful Bollywood dance numbers. Most probably, it's somebody's birthday, or a wedding, or a holy day.

The dogs next door suddenly erupt in fierce barking like it's a life or death issue, but as I'm about to get out of my cane chair to investigate, they abruptly stop. What was that all about?

In the old days, sannyasins lived all over Koregaon Park, some in the mansions themselves, some at the back in servants' quarters and some in bamboo huts hidden away in corners of big, rambling gardens. One guy built a tree hut, while others camped on open roofs and balconies. Everybody wanted to live as close as possible to the back gate of the Shree Rajneesh Ashram, as it was then called.

In 1977, I had a room upstairs in an old house and was paying the princely sum of 100 rupees a month in rent. In contrast, my current rent is 20,000 a month, which says a lot about inflation, the value of the rupee and my personal earning capacity.

Enough of reverie. The sun has slipped behind the house, the shadows are lengthening and it's time for tea in the resort. Funny, really, when I'm here, it's like I've never been away. Tomorrow is Monday and the traffic comes back...

Pune Diary 9

Cough control meditation

Nearly died in the Evening Meeting yesterday evening. It was a severe miscalculation on my part, because I thought I'd be okay, even though I was still a bit sick.

I was fine while waiting outside and when walking in with everyone else. The auditorium is big, square and cold, with a tall pyramid ceiling, a dark green marble floor and sound-proofed double-glazing on the windows. I've heard it referred to as 'the big fridge' because it seems rather stark and bare. But it's a great place to meditate, which, when you consider the fact that it has none of the atmosphere of ancient temples and other holy places, is a remarkable achievement.

I unrolled a long, black mat to insulate me from the cold floor, then placed one of those resort-style 'sitting meditation' chairs on top of it – basically, a square cushion with a strong back support. I sat down, then wrapped myself inside my big, warm, white shawl, feeling very cosy, ready for a deep, relaxing meditative experience.

Then, without warning, a sudden tickle in my throat quickly escalated into a massive need to burst out coughing, and I found myself mentally pleading with the musicians: "Come on, start the music NOW before I rupture my guts holding in this cough!"

In all these years, I've never had to leave the Evening Meeting because of coughing, but this time I was being severely challenged. Finally, when it seemed like I'd been holding my breath forever and making strange bodily heaving movements on my seat, the music started, but, to my dismay, with one of those long, solo violin intros – way too quiet to hide a cough.

Again, I was silently screaming at the musicians: "Where's the beat? Come ON!" Eternity passed before my eyes and then, at last... "Boom... boom..." in came the drums. Yay! Up went the noise level and from my throat emerged a muted, carefully orchestrated coughing-release session that continued all the way through the dancing phase.

Still, it seemed pretty loud to me and I was kinda surprised that nobody was tapping me on the shoulder and pointing to the exit, ordering me to leave.

Don't get me wrong, I appreciate the rule of silence in Osho Auditorium. After all, I didn't travel eight thousand kilometres to listen to a ninety-minute concert of throat-

clearing and coughing. The outer silence is needed to support my meditator's longing for inner silence. So when coughers get asked to leave, it's fine with me.

But, hey, it's a little different when it's my turn and on that particular evening I really didn't want to sit in the chilly, open-air welcome centre with the other invalids, watching an Osho video and wheezing along with everyone else.

Half-way through my 'I'm-not-really-coughing' meditation I turned around to check who was near me and... oh no! A senior resort guy was standing right behind me and it seemed impossible he hadn't heard my throat-clearing gymnastics, but he was busy operating the Wi-Fi pad that controls the auditorium's sound-mixer, so either he didn't notice, or didn't care.

The music climaxed in three shouts of "Osho!" and we all sat down in... well... yes... silence. Gently, I peeled open a Strepsil packet – cough sweet unwrapping noises are usually tolerated, although I did see one guy admonished for it – and sucked eagerly and lengthily on a lozenge.

Apart from having to wipe my nose frequently on my white shawl – forgot to bring the tissues – and mop tears from my eyes with the sleeve of my robe, everything went smoothly from then onwards. I wouldn't call it my best meditation exactly, but it certainly brought me into the present moment.

Pune Diary 10

The rich and the Raj

All the dogs in the universe gathered in Koregaon Park at 1:30 am last night to have an urgent and extremely noisy discussion, presumably about who was the alpha male. I have no idea what they decided, but the high-pitched yelps and squeals of the losers woke me up.

It's odd, their howls are so dramatic you'd think murder was being committed, but in the morning there are no mutilated bodies lying in the street. Just the usual, local, four-legged inhabitants, curled up and basking in the sunshine by the roadside.

Earlier last night, around 11:00 pm, I left the resort's Saturday night disco, walked out the back gate and noticed a big garden party in the Bajaj mansion located next door. Their property backs onto Lao Tzu House, where Osho used to live, and is also right behind the Basho swimming pool.

Bajaj is an Indian business family that's famous for making scooters, motorbikes, rickshaws and other cheap methods of transport. Clearly, their industrious endeavours have paid off, because it was Audis, BMWs and Mercedes that lined the road outside – not a rickshaw in sight.

Rather than waiting in their cars, the drivers were sitting together on the road for company, using sheets of newspaper to insulate their buttocks from the cold ground; a neat idea, although probably unsuitable for the Osho Auditorium.

The Bajaj mansion is typical of Koregaon Park's new look. The old bungalows from the days of the Raj had big sprawling gardens separated by low, crumbling walls and half-open gates with no watchman on duty. Nobody cared about security.

In marked contrast, the new ones have high walls topped with razor wire, monitored with CCTV and manned with 24-hour security. It's a new and unfriendly age, my friend.

Many of the old buildings have gone, which may seem odd because they were officially protected by the Pune Corporation for their historical and architectural value. But, well, you know how it goes: money changes hands, a big wall of metal sheets suddenly surrounds a property, large holes mysteriously appear in the old building to show it's no longer in a liveable condition, a row of temporary huts appears to house construction workers imported from Rajasthan... and off we go.

Still, there are a few classics left. One is a big white mansion on Lane 2, which looks like the White House in Washington DC, sitting in the luxurious splendour of a double-wide property with an amazingly beautiful garden. Legend has it the old man who owned it was so passionately against Osho that on his death bed he made his son swear never to sell the property to a sannyasin.

Another, funnily enough, is the Meera bungalow inside the Osho Resort, where the Galleria sells robes, which has a typical Raj-style open veranda surrounding the building on three sides, although I don't think any servant of the British Empire would have considered painting his bungalow black.

Maybe I should have mentioned it before: all buildings in the resort are black. It was one of Osho's little things... "Paint it black," he said. So we did. I'm not sure why he wanted it that way, but maybe it was for the soothing, overall visual effect of maroon-robed people, green vegetation and black buildings... a very aesthetic combination.

Meanwhile, my coughing control in the Evening Meeting continues to improve, although I dare not lay down in the 'let go' phase of the final meditation for fear that my throat and lungs will do exactly that...

Pune Diary 11

My ayah's magnificent mobile

I don't believe it. My ayah has a better mobile phone than me. I saw her sitting outside the house, on the front steps, flicking through the apps on a Samsung Galaxy, whereas mine is a smaller, lowlier, Samsung Duos.

"Is that yours?" I asked in surprise and she nodded happily. Well, I did read in *The Times of India* that more people in this country have mobiles than they do toilets.

The mobile culture here is huge, with 900 million

accounts. Every little store is an agent for service providers. Every salesperson is an expert in problem-solving. Every police station is swamped with forms registering new users.

But it's a low budget market. Most people don't use smart screens, just cheap little Nokias, so my ayah is clearly at the top of the range.

By the way, strictly speaking, the word 'ayah' means a nurse and caretaker for children – that's how the British used it while ruling this country. It was sannyasins who started calling their servants and cleaners 'ayahs' and somehow the word stuck.

For a while, back there in the late 80s and early 90s, a colonial atmosphere was re-created by European and American sannyasins who set up permanent, comfortable homes for themselves around Koregaon Park and that's when the ayah culture began for us.

We had servants to do cleaning and washing – sometimes cooking as well – and we would sit around the table, at lunch or tea time, discussing their virtues, or lack of them.

"My ayah is useless...," was a common complaint.

"You can be grateful if they don't totally destroy your clothes in the wash..." grumbled others.

In marked contrast, some sannyasins would smile with pleasure and murmur, "Oh, but my ayah is simply *wonderful*; she does *everything* for me..."

Many of us discovered an unpalatable truth, which didn't fit well with our attempts to be more friendly and democratic than our Imperial predecessors: if you were too nice to ayahs, they thought you were stupid, became lazy and stole things from your rooms.

Low caste women from nearby slum areas, such as

the so-called 'Indian Village' by the railway tracks, loved working for Westerners because it was such an easy, well-paid gig. As I recall, most of them were called either 'Rosie' or 'Rita'.

Stealing could somehow be managed without dismissal. For example, a son might come to 'help' his mother with the work, then money or valuable objects would suddenly disappear from the house. The son would be accused, the mother would weep and beg him to return the stolen goods, but he would refuse and disappear.

Then... what to do? To us, it seemed unfair to dismiss the mother for the son's wrongdoing, so life would continue as before.

Once, I had a gardener who, while I was distracted and talking with a friend, managed to race inside my room, snatch a wallet containing about 3,500 rupees and go back to work as if nothing had happened. I was so impressed by the audaciousness of his crime that I didn't do anything – except make sure my door was locked at all times thereafter.

Then there was Rosie who, when I was in charge of a four-bedroom flat, consumed so much washing powder I think she must have been supplying the whole of Indian Village. She was devastated when the apartment closed, because she knew she'd never get such an easy, lucrative job again.

Back to the present: I am intrigued by my ayah's magnificent mobile phone and curious how she got it, because she's an honest soul and therefore improper acquisition is not an option. Her English is not good, and my Hindi is worse, but somehow we manage:

"How long have you had it?" I ask.

"One year," she answers, proudly.

"Did a Westerner give it to you?" I inquire.

She shakes her head.

"Did the house owner buy it for you?" I persist.

"No... I buy... new... seven thousand," she reveals.

Clearly, being an ayah isn't a bad job. One might even describe it as an 'upwardly mobile' profession.

Pune Diary 12

The last white man

It's not often that I order four expensive chocolate cakes and buy drinks for my friends but today is an exception. Today, I'm launching my novel, *The Last White Man*, in Dario's Restaurant, behind Hotel Sunderban, and I'm nervous as a mother hen with a newly-born chick.

In spite of my neurosis, everything is going smoothly. The books have arrived on time from the printer, the waiters have given me a quiet corner of the restaurant with six or seven tables for my presentation, and even though the sky clouded over this morning it hasn't rained of my parade.

Guests trickle in from the resort next door and soon I'm busy signing copies of my book, while helpful friends serve cake and order tea, coffee and sodas – I thought champagne would send us all to sleep at 4:30 pm in the afternoon.

So then it's time for me to say something and I begin by posing the question "Why write a novel?"

Well, leaving aside the fact that I wrote a novel to see if I could write a novel, I've always felt that Koregaon Park would make a great backdrop for a love story and mystery thriller.

As I explain to my audience, I was toying with the idea even before writing *My Dance with a Madman* – the story of my life with Osho – which was published in 2010. In fact, back in 2007, I wrote a complete first draft of the novel, but then, feeling dissatisfied, put it out of my mind for five

years. It lay there, on the hard drive of my laptop, waiting patiently to be revived.

The story is about an Englishman who comes to India and goes through an intense process of transformation. Sounds familiar? Well, wait a moment... This isn't my sannyas story. It's an exploration of the power of love: how an ordinary Western businessman gets pulled out of his comfort zone when he falls for a beautiful, wealthy Indian woman.

Much of the drama takes place in German Bakery Lane, where Stephen Parkhurst - my main character - lives in a guest house called 'Happy Home', which some sannyasins may remember. Many of us stayed there, until it was remodelled as an upmarket hotel and re-launched as the 'Hotel Executive Residency'.

And, of course, for the romantic scenes, Osho Teerth Park provides a great setting, with secret night-time meetings amid the bamboo groves, hollows and statues. But I won't go into detail because it might spoil the book.

Meanwhile, next door to Dario's, the resort is gearing up for the annual New Year's dance party and the number of visitors is swelling. This is the peak of the high season, which, with any luck, will extend well into January before the numbers start to thin out.

I seriously doubt that I'm going to make it through until midnight this year, because my coughing rate tends to double every hour after sunset. But I'm in for a surprise: hanging out with friends, consuming a little alcohol, dancing my ass off... time flies and I walk home at 00:30. Somehow, this annual, global ritual of renewal and rebirth has to be observed.

Pune Diary 13

Tiny terror of the night

After one month in India I got my first mosquito bite. This is some kind of record and shows how few mosquitoes have been around, so far, during the cold season.

The tiny air-borne terror woke me up at 2:29 am, which is the reason why I'm writing this diary entry at 2:59 am. At first, emerging confused and groggy out of deep sleep, I couldn't figure why I'd woken up, but then I heard it... that familiar, soft, high-pitched whine ending in sudden silence as it landed somewhere on my exposed flesh.

Adopting Plan A, I reached out from under the covers and caught hold of my trusty mosquito zapper – the kind that looks like a plastic tennis racket with electrified metal 'strings'. I thumbed the 'on' switch, pressed the 'activate' button and waved it slowly in the darkness around my head, hoping to make lethal contact.

I was holding the zapper with my left hand, but the cunning little fellow had landed on my left elbow, so he remained completely safe from my efforts. Eventually, though, as it sucked my blood, I felt the bite and realized my mistake.

Shifting to Plan B, I staggered out of bed and switched on the main light, temporarily blinding myself and waiting patiently for my eyes to make the transition from darkness to near-daylight. I hate hurting my poor eyes like this in the middle of the night, but I have no choice.

Then, in slow motion, I cautiously re-approached my

bed, zapper in hand. Often, if they've sucked a little blood, mosquitoes get lazy and will stay near the scene of the crime instead of immediately flying off to some dark spot in the room where they are either invisible, unreachable, or both.

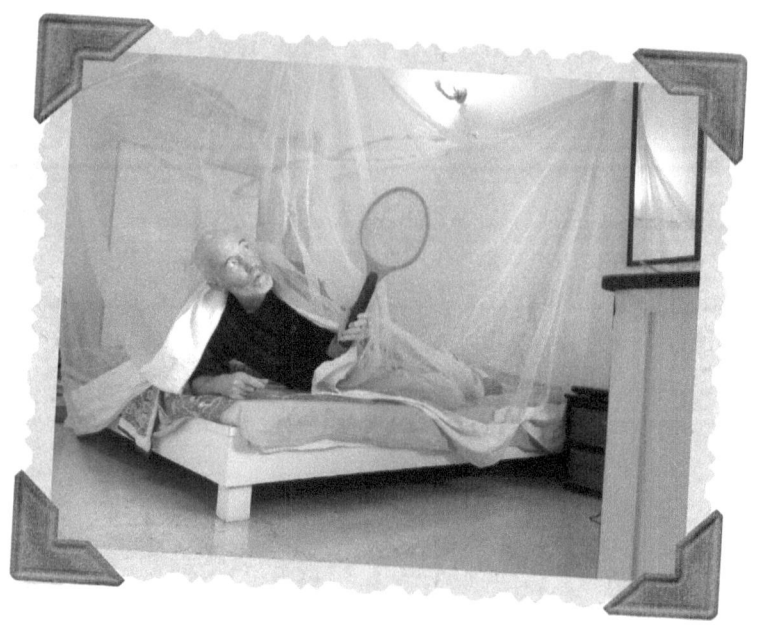

Yes! There he is, sitting on my spare pillow. Or, to be strictly gender-specific: there *she* is, because it's common knowledge that only the females suck your blood.

Now, patience is everything. In a kind of T'ai Chi rhythm of graceful slow motion, I come closer and closer to the bed, bringing the metal strings ever nearer to the small, dark target on my pillow. Now the racket is right above it... steady now... Whack! Sharply down on the pillow and a satisfying spark from the 'strings' signifies victory. Got it!

However, it's not the end of the story. Out of long experience, I know that sometimes these tough little critters survive the electric shock. They seem dead, but wake up after a few minutes and the whole drama begins again, so I feel compelled to crush it with my thumb. The flying vampire is now effectively disabled, if not completely deceased, and sleep is once again a possibility.

It's nice to sleep freely in an open room, but I know that, sooner or later, the number of mosquitoes will increase and I will need to fall back on my ultimate source of protection: a massive, king-sized mosquito net that has been with me for at least ten years.

I dislike the cone-shaped nets that hang from a single hook in the ceiling, because, down at pillow level, the netting is close to your face and it feels claustrophobic. So, I had this huge, square net made for me by Indo-Foreign Stores on MG Road.

Mostly, mosquitoes are just a nuisance, but occasionally, as we all know, they bring disease. Malaria is a rarity in this part of India, but dengue fever is quite common. If you've never had it, believe me, you don't want it. In addition to high fever, shivering and sweating, your whole body aches like crazy and you feel sore all over. Also known as 'breakdown fever', dengue lasts ten days and can occasionally be fatal although I've never known anyone die from it – even though, during the process, you sometimes wish you would.

So, all in all, a mosquito net is a good investment. It's now 4:30 am and I'd really like to get a little more shut-eye. Good night.

Pune Diary 14

Osho Dancing With Lady Gaga

Sophia's eyes light up with pleasure as she sees me coming up the stairs. "At last! Now I can pay you... I've been waiting

all this time." She consults her ragged notebook then digs into her purse and proudly hands over 500 rupees. "It's such a relief," she says, "Now please give me your email address before you go."

Sophia's bookshop is not exactly a secret, but its location – a small room, packed with books, accessed by a narrow fire escape, half-way up the back of a building – doesn't exactly smack the Pune public in the eye, even though it's just off busy North Main Road on Lane D.

It's a modest establishment, but you take your shoes off at the door... this is holy ground.

Sophia is a thin, elderly woman with glasses and she looks fragile but her eyes shine with a fierce love of books. Running this store gives her as much pleasure as Steve Jobs got from Apple.

I gave Sophia five books to sell for me, 3-4 years ago, then forgot about them. Only now, when I bring five more books – my new novel – can she settle accounts.

My next stop is to see Jagdish, who runs a bookshop on German Bakery Lane devoted exclusively to Osho. Jagdish has bright, twinkling eyes, a bald head and a wispy beard that make him look remarkably like his Master, or at least a distant cousin.

He used to be a political cartoonist in New Delhi and once drew a cartoon for me of Osho dancing with Lady Gaga, which I published as a book cover. I kid you not. It was a wild, impractical and short-lived idea, inspired by Lady Gaga's enthusiastic comments about Osho when she visited India in 2011.

Ms. Gaga, as you may recall, told reporters in Delhi that her favourite Osho book was about rebellion, and later tweeted to her fans she was "thinking of an Osho tattoo."

Thus inspired, I adapted my personal story about life with Osho and published the cloned book on Amazon, with the title 'Lady Gaga, This is Osho'.

Sanity soon prevailed, however, and I realized it was illegal to use Lady G's name without her permission and withdrew the book. But then a difficulty arose: Amazon wouldn't take the cover image off their internet website.

When Lady Gaga's managers in Los Angeles got to hear about it, they freaked. After all, when you're managing a $90 million-a-year pop star you don't want other people cashing in on her fame.

Overnight, I got a 'cease and desist' ultimatum from a

firm of New York City lawyers representing Gaga called, appropriately enough, 'Cashman' – don't you just love these New York names?

The letter was aggressive and intimidating, as one would expect NYC lawyers to be, and the reactions from my publisher and my internet promoter were predictable and identical: "The last thing we want is to be sued!"

But, as I pointed out to Cashman, there was no case to answer, because the book wasn't for sale anywhere in the world. The stubborn image on Amazon was the only remaining evidence of an extinct publication. They must've gotten the point and turned their legal guns on Amazon, because the image promptly vanished.

I wrote a dedication to Lady Gaga in *My Dance with a Madman* and sent her a copy to read. At the end of the dedication, I wrote: 'One more thing, Stefani, just for the record: it takes more than a tattoo to ride a tiger'. She has yet to reply.

By the way, I like Jagdish's cartoon and still keep it as a souvenir. Osho dancing with Lady Gaga – that would've been a sight to see.

Pune Diary 15

Dance Of The Rooms

I'm off to Goa for a couple of weeks, but I want to keep my room in Koregaon Park. This means I need join in the familiar 'Dance of the Rooms' routine that occurs regularly in Pune at this time of year, when everyone is juggling spaces and continuously changing their minds about where they want to go and what they want to do.

Sannyasins, by nature, are completely unreliable. It's not a bad thing. I rather like it – after all, I'm one myself. We mean well and have good intentions, and sometimes we actually do what we say we're going to do, but it all depends on our inner feeling and this can change any moment... or, indeed, every moment.

For this reason alone, I'd never employ sannyasins if I was a businessman. The stress of managing such in-the-moment employees would drive me crazy.

When I put out the news that my space is free for two weeks, a friend from Denmark immediately says 'Yes, I want it! Can you keep it for me, darling?' And I say 'sure', but days later she cancels, because another friend has offered for her to stay in the Shamsharan apartment complex on Lane B and she likes the company there.

Not to worry. Already, another friend of mine in Russia is announcing desperately on Facebook that her best friend is coming to Pune for the first time and can someone pleeeeeese find her a space... So I say 'sure' and it's fixed.

Then, for days, people come up to me in the resort and

say, 'Hey, I hear your room is free' and I say 'Sorry, it's taken' and they say 'Oh man, if only I'd known... I have this friend coming tomorrow...'

Early January is like this, because it's high season and people are coming and going in big numbers. By the end of the month, it's exactly the reverse and people are asking 'I've got this great room, does anyone want it?'

Meanwhile, another friend of mine from Sweden connects on Facebook and says 'Hey, Subhuti, I lived in that house for four years, can you find me the space?' And I say 'Sorry, no rooms' and he says 'Well, if anything changes, I have a friend in Pune who can give you the money right now!'

Anna from Russia shows up and she's really nice and loves the room, but she needs to change roubles, so I take her in a rickshaw to Shankar – I've dealt with him for ages – but he just smiles and shakes his head and says 'Sorry, nobody takes roubles'. I don't ask why.

So, off we go to the ATM in Sadhu Vaswani Hospital, next to the resort, and three of us cram into the little booth because somebody needs to explain to Anna what to do with her card... and yes! Out come the rupees and the deal is sealed.

Now, we just need to meet tomorrow morning, outside the resort's main gate, when I'll give her the key on my way to the airport. And hey, on my last evening in Pune I bump into my landlady who asks me, 'Do you know anyone who wants a room? Someone just cancelled her booking'.

It's the room next to mine, so I send a quick message to the guy in Sweden that he can live here after all. Man, is he ecstatic!

By now, we've all been through a very familiar sannyasin tango, or maybe it's a quickstep, called 'Dance of the Rooms' which nicely mirrors our seemingly chaotic go-with-the-flow lifestyle. It all turns out okay, as we knew it would... and I've just got time to pack. Don't forget the bathers and the sunblock.

Pune Diary 16

Sunset on the beach

I flew down with Air India, having sworn on my father's grave never to take the overnight bus again. I've been there, done that. I've had good bus rides, bad bus rides, freezing bus rides, bumpy bus rides – well, the rides are *always* bumpy, so that's no surprise.

The journey back is worse. I've had rides from Goa that end in pre-dawn darkness somewhere outside Pune, so you have to argue endlessly with ruthless rickshaw bandits who want to charge you five times the price of your bus ticket just to get you home.

In years gone by, a couple of friends of mine have been in serious Goa bus accidents and one of them, a dancer, had her legs mangled so badly that the fragments had to be literally screwed back together in a series of operations. Fortunately, she lived to dance again.

But it's not danger that turns me off. It just plain old discomfort.

I've also taken a taxi, a train and even – in the old days – a boat from Panjim to Mumbai, which was, of course, a slow and roundabout route but great fun. Now, though, at the tender age of 68, I opt for convenience and comfort. I fly.

As usual, I arrive in Goa full of intentions to check out new places. For example, I've never been to Agonda, in South Goa, which I'm told is lovely – 'like Goa used to be' before the arrival of several million tourists, including myself, who changed this place forever.

But, as usual, I find myself sharing a taxi from the airport and heading for Candolim, where I've been a dozen times before. The route is familiar: down the hill from the airport to the ocean, past the huge barges that carry iron ore from the mines, onto the main highway, by-passing Panjim and crossing two wide river estuaries before turning off through little fishing villages and narrow winding roads towards our destination.

Downtown Candolim is a tourist horror show, full of restaurants showing English football matches on cable TV and offering menus in Russian. But, as many sannyasins know, just beyond the town is a little dirt road – turn left at Julia Bar – which takes you down to the sea.

The great blessing of this track is that it stops short, so cars can't get to the beach. You have to walk half the

distance and this creates a bubble of serenity and relative isolation which sannyasins have come to love. And don't worry, the taxi drivers are accustomed to carrying your suitcase – for a handsome tip, naturally.

Passing through a grove of coconut palms, the track brings us to our sacred guest houses: Donna Florina, D'Mello's, Shanu, Sea Pearl and Villa Felix. Since I didn't book ahead of time, I won't get in any of them, but there are a few lesser-known ones, further back from the beach, and here I find a nice, clean room, complete with large bed and mosquito net. Good enough and relatively cheap. I'll take it, thanks.

By the time I've unpacked, it's around 4:00 pm and time to slip into a t-shirt and pair of shorts and walk down to the beach. The short hike takes me past Shanu and down a narrow, sandy path surrounded by bushes filled with chattering birds, opening out at the bottom onto the beach at Pete's Shack, where the Nepali waiters greet me like an old friend, shaking hands and laughing.

First, a dip in the ocean, which looks blue and welcoming even though – as all Goa enthusiasts know – it's not the cleanest sea in the world. But still, very refreshing on a hot day after a long trip.

Then, after towelling off, I return to Pete's and order a fresh-squeezed pineapple juice and a Nutella-coconut pancake to celebrate my arrival.

I'm in no hurry to hit the sunbeds. My skin needs to be fed sunshine in small, homeopathic doses or it freaks out badly, bubbling up in white spots and red pimples. It takes me about a month to get a decent suntan. I'll start on the sunbeds tomorrow morning.

Meanwhile, sunset brings many sannyasins down to the

shoreline and it's time for 'hello' hugs and meetings with people who I never usually see in Pune. The sun doesn't make it to the horizon, disappearing instead behind a purple haze, but I've made it to Goa and it feels good.

Pune Diary 17

Magnetic pull of the market

I have made a clear decision *not* to go to the Saturday Night Market. This gives me a strange feeling as I walk down to the beach, because I intuitively know that I'm going to meet people who will be going to the market and this will prove irresistible.

Sure enough, I run into two friends.

"Going to the market?" I inquire.

They nod. "Yes... coming?"

"Okay."

I yield to the magnetic pull the market exerts all along the Goa coast and we arrange to meet outside Lawande Supermarket, where we argue with local taxi drivers and end up paying 900 rupees for the trip.

The drive to Arpora is about 15 minutes, but, unbelievably, our local driver goes right past the market entrance as if he's heading for Arambol, so we have to shout "Stop, baba!"

My god! Can you believe it? I thought every taxi in India knew how to get to this place, it's so popular.

For me, it's essential to get to the market early, around 6:00 pm, when there are no lines of cars waiting to get in. Later, it's not an uncommon sight to see taxis backed up for one or two kilometres and sometimes impatient passengers get out and walk the final stretch.

At this early hour, stall holders are still arranging their wares: brightly-coloured dresses, scarves, shawls, quilts, saris, leather pants, rings, bangles, necklaces, gold and silver jewellery, chillums, psychedelic art, incense, sandals, scented teas, pirated movies and music...

I'm not really in the mood for shopping, so I enjoy watching the western women who come here to sell. They have a fashionable uniform of cool: lots of bare, sun-darkened skin, usually decorated with tattoos and skin piercings... piled-up Rasta hairdos... black tank tops, tight black mini-shorts with long bare legs or trendy ripped tights... in short, the ultimate hip Goa chick... some with slightly grey auras indicating regular use of intoxicating substances.

An Italian friend of mine, Letizia, is more conservatively attired and selling her rune decks, so I swap a copy of my new novel for a psychic reading. She says my book will be a success and a revolution is on the way financially. Hmm, does this mean I'll have money, or just learn to enjoy life without money? The cards don't say.

Another friend at the market is Akal, also Italian, who lives in Candolim and sells the most beautiful range of soft, cotton shawls I've ever seen. Her sense of colour combinations, mostly in pastel, is awesome.

After a slow cruise around the stalls, I meet another Italian – seems like it's in the stars tonight – but he's male and, like me, quickly tires of shopping. This is Krishna, an artist who, strictly speaking is Italian Swiss, and we have known each other for decades.

Krishna and I head for the market's food zone, where stallholders offer you an impressive variety of snacks and meals, ranging from pizza to pies, from chicken to cheesecake. We feast on momos, Kingfisher beer and fruit-filled crepes.

Live music is a feature of the Saturday Night Market and the opening act tonight in the central, open-air plaza features a local sitar and table player who are pretty good. Soon, however, they are replaced by an ancient American hippie who belts out the blues on his guitar. It's 7:30 pm and I'm done.

Struggling against the surge of people flooding in the gates, I run into Aviram, a German friend, and we share a very comfortable taxi back to Candolim, smiling with compassion as we zoom past the long line of cars crawling towards the market.

Soon, I'm on the beach, in Pete's Shack, enjoying the peace and quiet, sipping a ginger-lemon tea and listening to the ocean. Clearly, this is the best bargain I've found all evening.

Pune Diary 18

Sunrise on the beach

The crows are the first to wake. Sometime around 6:15 am they start cawing sleepily to each other through the trees and coconut palms. I'm also awake and soon slide out of my mosquito net, splash cold water on my face and head out the door, because dawn and sunrise is my favourite time of day.

The way to the beach is lit by a fading moon, hanging low over the sea and sending a silver pathway back to the beach in front of me. Behind me, the eastern sky is slowly getting lighter.

The Nepali boys who run the shack are still sleeping on the sunbeds, their heads and bodies entirely covered with shawls and blankets. But I'm not the first awake person on the beach. The early joggers are already running along the shoreline and these are mostly local Goans, who carry sticks to ward off the beach dogs.

To be fair, the dogs don't usually harass people and especially not at this hour, which is too early for them. When they do wake up, they're mostly busy checking out other dogs, or chasing the red Lifeguard jeeps that patrol the shoreline.

The first Westerners appear around 7:00 am: a group of hikers meet on the beach and shake hands in greeting, then stride off towards Baga, probably heading for Anjuna.

At 7:15, it's as if someone switches on an electric light: the clouds over the sea are suddenly lit up in pink and orange. The sun is almost up and now it gets rapidly lighter. More people are walking, jogging. The neighbourhood dogs are up and the ones who know me come over for a morning pat, wagging their tails in friendly greeting.

An elderly man practices Zen archery near Oceanic beach cafe, shooting arrows at a target in the sand, while a Russian spiritual teacher – dressed, of course, all in white – sits with her disciples in a small circle between Oceanic and Martha's.

There are sannyasin territories here: Italians congregate in two separate tribes, one at Oceanic and one at Martha's; Germans congregate at D'Mellos and the rest of us at Pete's, where we rub shoulders with Russian and British tourists.

Now the first sunbathers are coming down the slope from the guest houses, seeking out the best sunbeds and carefully marking them as reserved with towels and shawls.

Waiters from the shacks have already reserved the rest with towels given to them the night before by still-sleeping tourists. Soon all beds are taken and the sun hasn't yet hit the beach.

I stroll up and down the sand, close to the sea, watching the eastern sky until a large red ball of cosmic fire peeks over the coconut palms. Even though I know some of the other walkers, we don't stop and chat. It's too early for conversation.

I can't order breakfast yet. The Nepali boys are cleaning the tables, straightening the chairs, taking away the trash. I know the routine. At 8:00 am it's okay to sit down with my laptop and use the Wi-Fi, but not to order. They'll come and tell me when the kitchen is ready.

A paper boy arrives with *The Times of India*, bringing news of the world's madness. Now, one of the waiters approaches me and we both know what my order is going to be:

"Banana porridge with honey, papaya slice, black tea with hot milk separate."

The sun hits the beach and the day begins...

Pune Diary 19

Local villain, local hero

Garbage is the theme of the morning. As I sip meditatively on my cuppa, *The Times of India* informs me that local villagers near Assagao – just a few kilometres away – caught a man and woman unloading tons of garbage from a truck, hurriedly dumping it into bushes alongside the road between Baga and Anjuna.

I know the spot. You drive over a small hill covered in trees and bushes, enjoying the fact that you've finally escaped from traffic congestion, and suddenly you notice the roadsides are packed with garbage, including immense quantities of plastic bottles and plastic bags.

The police were called. The man confessed. He'd been hired by several Anjuna hotels to take away their crap with no questions asked. He was caught red-handed, but must've been a smart guy because he immediately transformed himself from villain to hero by making amends: he not only took away what he'd brought, but another five vanloads of other people's garbage.

Exactly where he took it, *The Times* does not reveal. One assumes the final destination was more legitimate. But, in any case, this noble gesture of atonement is of no more effectiveness than – if you'll excuse my crudeness – pissing into a hurricane. Why? Because this entire coastline is drowning in garbage.

To misquote the Bard, "There's something rotting in the State of Goa." Except, of course, plastic doesn't rot.

Even here, behind our very own chai shack, the pleasantly green shrubbery conceals piles of garbage and, in plain sight, plastic bags and other detritus are scattered in open spaces. Occasionally, a local cow can be seen methodically chewing pages of newspapers – at least one species on this planet can find a proper use for them.

Goa's politicians simply don't know what to do. Or, rather, they know what to do, but they won't spend the money to do it. Instead, the money goes into their pockets.

I'm not kidding. It is widely believed by the rest of India that Goa is the most corrupt state and, in a country where corruption is the way of life, that's a difficult reputation to sustain.

Even as I sit in front of my shack, enjoying the early morning, looking out across a calm, blue Indian Ocean, waiting for breakfast, a column of smoke is rising between our shack and the next. One of the owners is burning garbage. It's prohibited, but it happens.

Fortunately, the offshore breeze takes the smoke straight across the beach and out to sea, but if I was walking briskly along the shoreline – as many tourists do, for morning exercise – I would be inhaling generous quantities of dioxins from burning plastic.

The Goa Herald, which I also bought this morning, offers news of a garbage treatment plant in the village of Canacona. The equipment recently burned down, so now the garbage being shipped into the corporation's walled site is being secretly burned – according to the report.

"No it isn't," insists a Canacona official, because burning is illegal. But then a journalist slipped inside the compound and photographed employees setting fire to mounds of garbage. When shown irrefutable evidence, the same Canacona official assured the journalist "I will see that such a practice is immediately stopped."

Nevertheless, the burning continues. This is how it goes.

Hotels built on the Northern bank of the Baga River release their sewage straight into the river, according to Desmond Oliveira, one of the few environmentalists in the area. He protests that the river is being destroyed, but the only response from local officials is to issue more building permits for more hotels to be built.

"We are shouting but nobody's listening," is the common cry among the few environmentalists who live along the coast. It's a David and Goliath situation, but Goliath is winning.

"Goa is finished," pronounces an old Frenchman

dismally, as he sips his coffee at a table next to mine, folding his newspaper in an act of finality, like a doctor giving up on an expired patient. He's an artist who's been living here for 35 years.

In spite of all this, I must say I'm having a good time. And we can take heart from the fact that, even in its currently overcrowded condition, Goa can always get worse. Now its politicians are talking about creating a new airport in North Goa to bring in another one million tourists per season. Unbelievable.

Pune Diary 20

Waste disposal on trotters

"I really don't know why I come here to sunbathe in a garbage dump," sighed one old friend, as she lay topless on her sunbed, eyeing the rubbish behind her, scattered among the creepers and bushes.

"Sure you do," I countered. "It's still the best place to relax and do nothing."

"Hmm... I guess so," she mused, sipping meditatively on a fresh-squeezed pineapple juice. "I can't help remembering how it used to be..."

For me, the present is way too interesting to spend time kissing the past's backside. But still, like my friend, I'm occasionally reminded of the old days, back in 1977, when there was one small guest house on this whole stretch of beach. If you didn't want to stay there, you could rent a room from a Goan family, or pay a local handyman to build a hut for you among the coconut palms.

Sunbeds? Not one. If you wanted shade, a few rupees would translate into four poles stuck in the sand with a makeshift roof made of palm leaves.

It was then that I made acquaintance with Goa's unique sanitation system. I was staying in a small room at the rear of a family bungalow. There was no bathroom. Outside my door, a plastic hosepipe snaked up to a shower head nailed to a wooden post, where I could wash in semi-privacy, thanks to surrounding shrubs, bushes and overhanging branches.

To take a dump, I had to cross a raised patio and squat

over a hole, which allowed my deposit to fall to the bottom of the patio wall, on the ground beneath. There was no toilet paper. You washed your bum with water from a metal cup, using your left hand – that's why all Indians, until recent times, ate food only with the right hand. It was simple division of labour.

What puzzled me, though, was that there was no sign of any previous deposits on the ground below the hole. Strange! This wasn't a new toilet. In fact, it looked old enough to precede the Raj. Anyway, on the first morning of my stay, I shrugged off this puzzle, dropped my pants, squatted over the emptiness and pretty soon evacuated my bowels – not a difficult task when you have stomach trouble.

Having washed off, I stood up and hoisted my pants. Almost immediately, there was a grunting noise on the dirt track winding through the trees beyond the patio and pretty soon two large porkers came trotting along. The lead pig didn't pause, but the second one stopped, raised his snout in the air and inquisitively sniffed the breeze. He turned towards my house and with unerring accuracy zeroed in on my small, steaming pile and gobbled it up.

Now that's what I call recycling. I was alarmed to learn that the locals were eating these pigs, especially on celebration days, such as weddings, but... well, that really wasn't my problem was it?

Alas, this 100 percent natural, certified organic, eco-friendly method of waste disposal has been unable to keep up with demand. There just aren't enough pigs to consume the deposits of Goa's annual influx of 2.6 million tourists.

There wasn't any plastic garbage in those days, but it was a mixed blessing. A lot of us used to get sick... very sick. We used to get boils on our legs and in our armpits. We used to get amoebic dysentery, turning our bowels into rivers, making us look thin and spiritual. We used to get hepatitis, turning the whites of our eyes a deep, romantic yellow. We would lie for days, sometimes weeks, in our little bamboo huts, waiting for the sickness to run its course, with barely enough strength left to roll a joint.

The introduction of filtered water, packaged in handy one-and-five-litre plastic bottles, transformed the health situation. The downside is, of course, that these containers, once emptied of their health-giving content, litter the ground everywhere.

It's strange, kinda ironic, that if I'm going to point my finger at anyone for the state of Goa today, I'd have to include myself. I wasn't one of the first hippies to descend on Anjuna Beach in the late 60s and early 70s, but I joined them a little later.

We discovered the beauty of Goa. We spread the word. Following us, in the early 80s, came the first charter flights from Germany, but they were soon overtaken in numbers by the British working class, especially those without seasonal jobs in winter – like construction workers – who suddenly realised they could live more cheaply in the sunshine than they could in the dismal weather at home.

Scandinavians followed and then, as the Iron Curtain crumbled into dust, Russians started making an appearance – the mafia came first, because they had the money, bringing with them models and call girls. Last, but certainly not least, came the newly-enriched, rapidly expanding, Indian middle class.

Well, historically, that's not quite accurate; even back in the 70s there was one regular tour from Mumbai, when an enterprising businessman offered coach trips to Arambol for Indian men, with the promise of seeing naked hippies lying on the beach. Usually, they weren't disappointed.

I must confess, when I made my first bus trip from Pune to Goa I was fantasizing about sex on the beach with a naked hippie girl. As fate and fortune would have it, my dream came true in a small cove near Vagator, where we made love on the sand, hidden between two rocky outcrops. We had to hide, not only for modesty's sake, because this sweetly available young woman had left her boyfriend stoned out of his mind in a hut some 200 metres away.

But I was in for a surprise: when my partner put on her clothes at the end of the day, they were orange. She was also a sannyasin!

"Ah, that Pune energy!" she sighed, contentedly squeezing my hand.

I didn't know whether to feel grateful or ripped off.

Pune Diary 21

Goa face scrub

In the early morning, two bodies wash ashore on the beach, just south of Calangute. They are identified as a young pregnant woman and her husband, vacationing from Delhi, who drowned yesterday afternoon while playing together in the sea.

It's a sad moment, but not uncommon here on the beaches of Goa. Many young Indians come here, with no previous experience of the ocean and no swimming skills. They jump around in the water, having a great time, then someone gets knocked over by a wave and is tumbled around by the surf.

At this point, panic is the enemy. In those few seconds underwater, when it's not clear what's up and what's down, it's all too easy to struggle against the movement of the sea, then gulp lung-fulls of water, lose consciousness and drown. Apparently, in this case, the wife got knocked over, the husband tried to help her and they both went under.

Some casualties are foreigners, especially those who have been drinking steadily through the day before jumping in the water. Some rescue agencies say up to 90 percent of those who drown in Goa have alcohol in their blood.

We think the ocean is for entertainment, but it demands respect. I should know. I had an embarrassing accident here last year, in front of my favourite chai shack, shortly after arriving in Goa.

Return with me and imagine the scene:

It's about 5:30 in the afternoon and the sea is a little rough, as is often the case at this time of day when the wind is blowing strongly onshore. But, for me, it's no problem. I was brought up on the South Coast of England, swimming in the English Channel. I'm used to rough seas.

I've been swimming for about half-an-hour and am heading back towards the beach, looking behind me for a wave to body-surf and carry me to the shore. Perversely, at this moment, there are no big waves, so I keep edging closer to the beach while looking over my shoulder to see if a roller will come before I need to walk out.

I'm already inside my depth when a big wave surges up behind me. Instinct tells me it's way too late to ride a wave like this, but, suppressing all my nautical alarm bells, I decide to enjoy one more ride. I stretch out my arms in front of me, holding my body straight like an arrow, and

ride the breaking crest.

What a dumb thing to do. Next thing I know, my legs are being flipped up in the air, while my head is being thrust strongly downwards. Bang! My face hits the sand and my neck takes the impact, twisting to the side. For a few seconds, I'm rolled around in the surf like I'm inside a washing machine, but I have enough sense not to fight it. I just go with the motion and pretty soon the wave has exhausted itself on the beach. I have time to stand up before the undertow drags me back.

When I touch my face to examine the damage, my hand comes away covered in blood. Cosmetically speaking, my forehead and nose have just enjoyed an in-depth face scrub. It's a superficial wound, I know, but looks dramatic and the last thing I want on this busy beach is to be surrounded by well-wishers and do-gooders trying to help me. First aid around here might be more threatening to my health than the accident itself.

I try to wash off the blood before coming out of the sea, but more blood just keeps coming, so I walk quickly up the beach, passing the sunbeds and the shack, ignoring questions like "What happened to you?" and head for my room. On my way, I grab my backpack from my sunbed and pull out a purple scarf which I throw over my face like I'm a female refugee from Afghanistan who hasn't yet realised she can take off her *burka*.

Reaching the sanctuary of my room, I enter the bathroom, shower off, and then inspect the damage. My god, I look a sight. Deep scrapes have ripped skin and flesh off my forehead and my nose. Blood is dripping down into my beard. I look like the Elephant Man having a bad face day.

I know this kind of wound will heal quickly, but my main concern is infection. Back in the old days, this was a hazard for the entire hippie community. Without treatment, a tiny cut on a toe could result in a swollen foot in no time.

In those days, my main ally was iodine, a strong disinfectant that makes a bright yellow stain on your skin, which, of course, makes the wound look even worse. But it's effective and also dries the wound, helping to form a healing scab.

Throwing my veil over my face once more, I head for the chemist shop on the main road and ask for a bottle of iodine. The young sales assistant eyes me curiously, wondering who is lurking behind the *burka*, but senses the urgency of my request and quickly hands over a bottle of Betadine.

For a moment I'm confused. "Is this iodine?" I quiz her.

"Yes, yes, iodine, best quality," she insists, so I hand over the money and walk back to my room.

The bleeding is slowing. I take out a clean cotton pad, pour iodine on it and gently dab the scrapes on my face. Ouch! The sting is sharp and strong, but carries the promise of problem-free healing. Now there's nothing to do except lie on my bed and wait for nature to bring back my face.

Pune Diary 22

Waves a-coming in...

Rain shower ending
Even the dogs are silent
The night grows deeper

It's not often a haiku pops into my head, but an unseasonal thunderstorm has rolled along the Goa coast tonight, bringing a heavy shower of rain, leaving coolness and silence in its wake. It is four o'clock in the morning and very, very quiet.

Not even the dogs are barking, whereas earlier they were howling with such sad, mournful cries it made me wonder if they'd been watching a programme about Canadian timber wolves on Discovery Channel.

It's too soon for the crows to begin their pre-dawn chat show. All I can hear is the softly booming sound of surf along the shore and the occasional "splat!" of a large drop of water falling from tall coconut palms onto the leaves of bushes outside my window.

A flicker of headlights dances among the trees and I hear a vehicle approaching. A gate opens and there's the unmistakeable sound of a suitcase being dragged along a path towards a taxi. Must be Deven. He's heading for the airport, catching an early morning flight to Delhi, then flying on to Dehradun, the closest airport to his final destination, Rishikesh. There, he will meet his Italian girlfriend and play music for a school of orphans, run by a friend of ours.

Deven is a fifty-something sannyasin who in his youth used to be a pop singer in Germany. Blond, tanned, wielding an acoustic guitar and wowing the audience with his energy, he's still a good performer. That's why, yesterday evening, about 100 of us crowded into the courtyard of his little house to sing Osho songs, mixed with a smattering of rock 'n roll.

The atmosphere is casual and good-natured. The evening wasn't planned more than a couple of days earlier and no notices were put up. But the sannyasin bush telegraph is effective and word gets around. There probably aren't more than 200 sannyasins in the whole of Goa and they are scattered thinly along the coast – some I never see – but somehow everyone keeps in touch with everyone else.

Accompanied by a second guitar and a hand-held *djembe* drum, Deven warms up the crowd with some easy, lively songs before moving into more spiritual stuff. Then he introduces one of my favourite songs that was born in the Pune ashram in the 70s, adapted from an ancient song by Kabir, India's most celebrated poet-mystic:

There is so much magnificence, near the ocean,
Waves a-coming in, waves a-coming in...

Kabir is referring to the inner ocean, that infinite space that opens up inside us when the mind is silent and the tiny 'self' dissolves into the welcoming arms of eternal nothingness.

This may sound like spiritual romanticism but it used to happen to us, when Osho was alive, especially during music group, when every night we'd gather in the meditation hall to sing our hearts out. The power of Osho's presence was so strong and the sense of devotion – generated by hundreds of people singing – so intense that we'd actually experience what Kabir was talking about in his magical poetry.

Even now, nearly forty years later, we can taste the same space together when we sing these songs and that's what brings us here, to Deven's little courtyard. It's as if we've all been carrying the quality of ecstasy within us, all this time, and we just need an excuse to reawaken it.

The men begin, singing Kabir's words, generating a groundswell of energy that slowly builds as we move deeper into the feeling of the song. Then, after a while, the women's voices come in high above us, with a sweet, delicate, soaring harmony of "Alleluia," repeated softly over and over again. In this simple way, our hearts open and spiritual communion happens.

Deven has a fine sense of balance. When he feels the atmosphere is getting too holy he abruptly changes our mood by leading us into a raucous, unspiritual pop song like *Twist and Shout* by the Beatles. We laugh and enjoy going crazy as we sing the classic "aaah... aaah... aaah" that builds higher and higher, louder and louder, ending in that famous scream.

I recognized, a long time ago, that working on myself would have to continue after Osho died. While he was alive, the field of energy generated by his presence was so strong it was impossible for me to figure out my own spiritual state. We were flooded by his energy. Only when he'd gone could I get an unassisted reality check on the depth of my meditation.

That's why, whenever somebody asks me about my spiritual growth, I simply reply, "It's work in progress." Not *work* exactly, but words tend to lose their utility in this dimension. More like an ongoing exploration.

So, with no end in sight, I may as well enjoy the ride, hence my delight in singing.

Pune Diary 23

The Wednesday pilgrimage

It's 7:30 am on Wednesday morning and I'm waiting on the beach for my ex-girlfriend. We have promised each other to walk all the way from Candolim to Anjuna, where, as everyone knows, on this morning, every week, the massive flea market will be welcoming us.

She's only ten minutes late... not bad... and we set off along the shore.

We're in luck. The tide is out and we have flat, hard sand to walk on. At high tide, it can be awkward, because you have to walk on sloping soft sand, one foot higher than the other... kinda limping all the way to Baga. Not today, thank you.

As we pass Calangute we are greeted by lots of Indian tourists, mostly men, sipping early morning cups of chai. Some are in bathers and run into the surf with loud, enthusiastic shouts of glee. Once in the water, they look a little lost, as if they don't really know what to do – bathing is a relatively new leisure activity for most Indians.

A few Indian women stand in the surf, fully clothed, holding hands and shrieking in fear and delight as the waves hit them.

Leaving Calangute behind, we continue north along the beach and reach the Baga River about an hour after starting out. Here, in the old hippie days, we used to wade across at low tide, carrying our bags on our heads, to avoid the long trek inland to the nearest bridge. But a new bridge, just a few hundred metres inland, makes this unnecessary.

Once across the bridge, we turn left and seek out a narrow footpath that looks unpromising, a bit like someone's private pathway. But, if I remember rightly, this tiny track will take us up the hill that separates Baga from Anjuna.

This looks like it. I try to recall all the twists and turns, as civilization disappears behind us and we find ourselves climbing steadily among wild cashew trees and dense foliage.

Yes! Coming over the top, we walk through open fields of brown, sunburned grass and can see the Anjuna coastline unfolding below us... blue ocean, green palms... a stunning view. We also see, packed together by the beach, the temporary roofs of the stall holders that make up the flea market.

On the other side of the hill, we find the old, red, stone steps that take us down to our first destination: the famed Anjuna German Bakery. We walk through the back entrance into a big open dining area, protected from the sun by a ceiling of colourful strips of cloth.

It's already crowded, but we manage to find a nice table and order mineral water, coffee, muesli and croissants. For me, this is the best part of the trip. It's soooo satisfying to come in here and enjoy a good breakfast after a two-hour walk.

We take our time, ordering more coffee and snacks... then it's time to pay and head for our second destination: the big, sprawling, chaotic flea market.

As we wander between the stalls, the ear cleaners approach us and offer to take wax from our ears. Ha! That scam worked on me once, 20 years ago. They hide a little

ball of brown wax in their hand, so they can show you how much they're taking out of your ear and charge you several hundred rupees for their expert medical attention. Not today, thank you.

Even though I nearly buy several useless things, I'm not in need of anything and wait patiently for my friend to finish her shopping. Suddenly, she realizes she's had enough. I pat myself on the back for my strategy, having said nothing until she's the one who exclaims, "My god, I'm exhausted! Let's get out of here... now!"

No problem, my dear. 'Taxi!' (We're not going to walk back).

Pune Diary 24

Brahman bull among the sunbeds

It's 10:30 in the morning and I'm heading for my sunbed on the beach when I see a big Brahman bull standing under the sunshade roof, which is made of palm leaves. He's wedged himself in between my sunbed and the one next door and his horns are long and sharply-pointed.

Like the dogs, bulls and cows are a feature of beach life. I have no idea if they belong to anyone, or if they've been abandoned here by farmers and owners who no longer want them.

Anyway, the presence of these bovine beach-dwellers is tolerated by the guest house and restaurant owners, so here they are.

Other tourist and sunbathers are watching the bull, some taking photos, some ready to run. Hmm... don't fancy lying there with him standing next to me. I pick up one end of the sunbed and shift it noisily, cramping his space while trying to stay at a safe distance from his horns. The bull gets the message and slowly ambles away, out into the sunshine, but not far.

I lie down, keeping an eye on him. Sure enough, the sun gets too much for him and he wanders back. I flick my towel in his face, staying well away from the business end of his body, but it's no good. He's in between the sunbeds again. He's not a mean-looking fellow, but definitely has a stubborn streak in his character.

Okay, no more Mr Nice Guy! Staying on the other side

of the sunbed, I lean across and give him a good punch on his rump and yes, he's on the move again. This time I follow him, as close as I dare, herding him away from the sunbeds and across the open sand in front of the shack.

"Keep going, buddy! That's right!" I encourage him.

"Don't send him here!" a cry of alarm from my Swiss friend, Amira, who's been watching the whole drama from the next row of sunbeds, on the other side of the shack.

But I'm helpless, I have to keep him moving or he'll come back, and, sure enough, he wedges himself into the shade, right next to her sunbed.

Well, he's out of my territory, so I don't feel the same compulsion to risk life and limb by trying to move him again. Several people gather round to take photos. No one seems in a hurry to assist poor Amira, but she knows what to do, calling out "Ram! Help!"

Ram is the senior waiter in Pete's Shack and responds

immediately, walking fast towards the bull and making grunting noises which send a clear message "Move it, buddy!" Ram's done this a million times before and the bull knows the game is up.

He walks away from the sunbeds, behind the shack and out of sight. Mission accomplished.

"Thanks Subhuti!" says Amira, with just a trace of sarcasm in her voice. I wave cheerily and we all relax. Time to catch some rays...

Pune Diary 25

Chinmaya's concert

"He looks a bit like I've always imagined Jesus Christ to be," whispers Sarah.

Hmmm... I bet that's the first time my friend Chinmaya has been compared to Our Lord and Saviour. True, he has masses of hair, with thick tussled locks falling down to his shoulders and a long straggly beard, so conceivably he could play the lead role in a Passion Play. Dressed in a scarlet silk *kurta* top, with white cotton baggy pants, he does look rather divine tonight as he sits on a little makeshift stage, playing his *sarod*.

But there are certain aspects of Chinmaya that clearly set him apart from the Only Begotten Son. He smokes roll-your-own cigarettes, grew up in England and is over 50 years old -- as I recall, JC didn't make it past 33. Chin does, however, have a Jewish wife, born in Israel, who is beautiful enough to pass for Mary Magdalene.

Sarah is impressed. She and her friend Penelope have come with me tonight to Assagao village to enjoy this little concert. It's a delightful location, set in the garden of a lovely old Goan bungalow with decorative fairy lights hanging from the trees around the stage.

Flashback: I meet Sarah and her friend Penelope on the beach in front of Pete's Shack. They are lovely women, both around 50 years old, freshly arrived from the UK. The fact that they were sunbathing topless, adding grace and charm to the view, obviously had nothing to do with my enthusiasm for introducing myself.

Sarah is an impish-looking strawberry blonde, a real livewire, with tons of bubbly energy. As we chit-chat, she quickly becomes interested in Osho and his sannyasins. "I've always wondered how people get mixed up in a cult like that," she says brightly, "So, tell me, what was his flaw? I mean, as far as I can see, all of these cult leaders turn out to have a fatal flaw, don't they?"

"I think his biggest flaw was to invite people like me to become his to sannyasins," I reply jokingly, enjoying Sarah's innocent lack of diplomacy.

Penelope is the quieter of the two. She's been coming to India for the past eleven years and already knows about sannyasins.

I invite them to Chinmaya's concert in Assagao village. They happily agree and we meet after sunset on the main road.

"Do you know Assagao?" I ask a taxi driver. He nods enthusiastically.

"*Kitna*... how much?" He holds up two fingers – 200 rupees – and I nod agreement. But, of course, he doesn't know Assagao and soon we're stopping every kilometre so he can ask directions, while the amount he wants to charge rises by a hundred rupees each time.

"Very long way... very far... petrol expensive... taxes have gone up..." His psychological fare meter is working overtime, but we stop his mental clock at 400 and refuse to pay more, even if we have to drive all night.

To my relief, I spot Chinmaya standing by the roadside, smoking a cigarette and holding his cute little daughter in his arms.

Before I can leave the taxi and greet my musical friend, a long and useless negotiation is required, in which I try to persuade the driver to pick us up when the concert ends. But he wants 1,500 for the whole deal – bringing us and taking us home – which is clearly outrageous. So I pay him 400 for the one-way trip and wish him a good life.

Pretty soon we're all relaxing in the warm darkness, listening to the concert, which Chinmaya modestly describes as "a bit like an upscale variety show." He keeps changing musicians and styles, which is good for me since, like shopping, I have a short attention span for musical performances.

He's done a great job in assembling talent. There's a *tabla* player from Delhi, a local *ghazal* singer, two young Westerners who sing devotional *mantras* and a guy playing a flying saucer – a very strange-looking metal percussion instrument, with a wonderful sound, called a *hung*. Another long-haired musician plays the *santoor*, tapping out an exquisite tune on dozens of strings with two spoon-like sticks. Chinmaya plays the *sarod*, a kind of fretless guitar that is hugely popular in Northern India.

The whole thing is beautiful to watch and the quality is high. I feel touched that Chinmaya has the time, enthusiasm and energy to arrange these little concerts, which ought to be watched by thousands of people but attracts no more than a hundred.

He lives in Goa year-round, earning a modest living from his own music, helping out with other bands and adding his skills to various recording sessions. He gets by quite well, as indeed do many gypsy-like sannyasins.

It's a mystery, really, how those of us who love India somehow manage to live here, year after year.

Pune Diary 26

Reluctant meditator

This morning, I have to go and check on Prabhudasi, a friend from Hamburg, who cut her foot in the ocean yesterday.

She'd been in the sea a long time and was swimming towards the beach, intending to return to her sunbed. Thinking she was now in shallow water and could stand up, she put her foot down, expecting to feel sand. What she found was a broken glass bottle lurking in the shallows. The cut was long and deep. Now she's confined to her room, with a stitched-up foot and a generous supply of antibiotics.

"I'm *zoooo* glad you came! It gets *zoooo* boring here by myzzzelf," she greets me, opening her arms wide for a warm hug, while carefully balancing her bandaged foot on a chair next to her bed – she's been told to keep it up.

"It vas a big drama, ja? Just to arrive at der hospital... you voodn't beleef der problems. Tank god I vasn't alone... " Prabhudasi launches into a detailed and bloody account of her rescue, including a ride in a local lifeguards' jeep that she thought was taking her to hospital, but which stopped where the beach ended and the road began. Apparently, the vehicle wasn't supposed to leave the shoreline, so she was forced to hobble across the street to a regular taxi to complete the journey.

Of course, she'd left all her clothes in her room, so she soon found herself lying naked on a hospital bed --

well, *almost* naked -- having her foot stitched, while large numbers of locals watched at the emergency room door.

"Vill you close der door or not?" she cried at the staff, but apparently this had never been done. Intense humidity from the yearly monsoon had rusted the door in its open position. But Prabhudasi is not a woman to be denied, so eventually two burly medical orderlies heaved it almost shut.

Big, blonde and buxom, Prabhudasi takes up a lot of space – energetically that is – so it's fortunate she occupies the biggest room in her guesthouse, just behind the beach, not far from my own. Her door is always open for visitors, including her favourite beach dog.

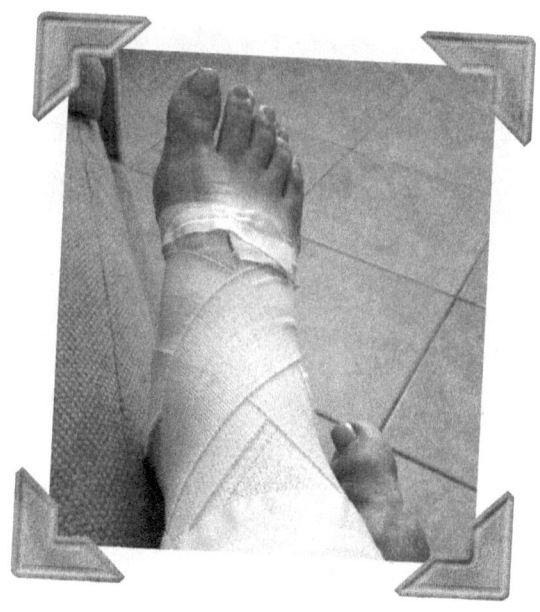

Prabhudasi is well cared for by her friends, who bring her presents and food. I notice, lying on her bed, an Osho book titled *The Hidden Harmony – Discover Your Inner Beauty*. There's a time for everything, especially when you're suddenly immobilized.

Perhaps there is karmic good fortune in her accident. In her normal healthy state, this forty-something, former hippie-girl is a tireless party animal. She's always on the go, running up and down the coast to the hotspots, dancing in all the discos. She has a great excuse: she's the main organizer of one of Germany's oldest annual trance parties and has to keep up with the latest trends.

Now an unexpected collision with a broken bottle, part of Goa's insoluble garbage problem, has forced her to lie on her bed and do nothing.

Meditation comes in strange ways.

Pune Diary 27

Goa full moon party

If someone invites you to a Full Moon party in Goa you will immediately envision crowds of semi-naked young people, high on drugs, dancing all night long to loud music on the beach, ceasing only after sunrise when pangs of hunger drive them off the dance floor to eat breakfast.

I used to go to those parties – the last one by accident. About 12 years ago, when my midlife crisis was forcing me to spend time with women much younger than myself, I was staying in Arambol with a lovely 27 year-old Dutch woman. We'd met in Pune and come to Goa for a honeymoon. After a long day on the beach, dinner in a local restaurant and love-making by moonlight on the sand, we were in bed, cuddling in a relaxed, sleepy way, ready for several hours of blissful unconsciousness.

Suddenly, at full volume, the unmistakeable *duff-duff-duff* of the trance beat came crashing into our room at full volume. I leapt out of bed and rushed outside, ready to verbally assault whatever neighbour had thoughtlessly turned his sound system up so high, when I saw the twinkle of fairy lights, hanging among a grove of coconut palms between our hotel and the beach.

That was the source of the music. A full-on trance party had been organized right outside our door. I went back inside and pulled on my pants.

"Get up, sweetheart," I told my friend. "We might as well join the party because there's no sleep for us tonight."

So that's what we did. I didn't spend much time dancing because I didn't like the wired-and-wasted look of the hairy creatures shuffling robot-like on the dance floor. I preferred to hang out and gossip with a young crowd who were sitting together on a big straw mat, rolling joints and drinking endless cups of chai supplied by enterprising local women. I turned down the magic mushrooms, though, not wishing to entirely lose my mind.

"You have beautiful eyes," said a young woman sitting next to me, as we looked at each other for the first time, which, as I'm sure you'll agree, is a nice way to say 'hello'. She told me her name was Marlise, from Sydney, and introduced her friends – a mixed group of Australians, Americans and Brits, all in their early 20s. My girlfriend and I were with them until daybreak, smoking, drinking chai and exchanging traveller's tales.

Those kinds of parties still happen, but I have a feeling the one to which I've been invited on this full moon night is going to be a little different.

Devena picks me up an hour after sunset. She's in her late fifties, with penetrating blue eyes, short brown hair, tons of youthful vigour and a deep Goa tan. She lives in Germany but creates long breaks for herself each winter, setting up a studio on the porch of her guesthouse in Candolim and letting loose her creativity as a painter.

By the way, I must apologize for the way I keep on introducing new people into this journal, but that's just how my life is. People come and go all the time.

Devena sets off along the beach, me in tow, and after a while turns inland, weaving her way through a series of badly-lit streets and dark alleyways.

"There's usually dogs along here at some point," she warns me. "One night, I was cornered here by five or six of them, all barking madly at me. They wouldn't let me go for half-an-hour."

Great. Right on cue, a low growl in the darkness, off to my right, suggests an imminent attack, but obviously we did not intrude sufficiently on the animal's territory. He lets us go with a snarl and a couple of half-hearted barks.

"There's a ditch here," advises Devena, flashing her unsteady beam close to my right foot.

Whoa, that was close. I nearly put my foot in a black hole.

"And there's some sharp metal here..." We cautiously ease our way between two tall, jagged sheets of rusted steel to gain access to another path.

I still retain this image, from years back, of walking to parties through open, picturesque glades of coconut palms, their tall trunks and spikey-leaf crowns standing in silent, serene splendour in the moonlight. This feels more like the backstreets of Mumbai.

A few minutes later, to my relief, we arrive undamaged at a villa with a large garden. A bonfire is blazing vigorously in an open space in front of the house, which seems a little bizarre considering the air temperature is well over 20°C, but nevertheless it gives the place a cosy feeling.

We're not the first to arrive. About thirty people are already here and I notice they're all over 60. Some are pushing 80. I'm not really surprised, but I have to smile. These are the party animals with whom I'm going to celebrate the full moon?

It is for this reason that younger sannyasins, living in social hotspots like Anjuna and Arambol, like to refer to our scene in Calangute as 'Jurassic Park' – implying we're so old we belong to that distant period in the planet's history. In short, we are dinosaurs.

Santosh, our host, is almost 80 but he's working like a 25 year-old. He's built a clay oven in the shape of a turtle, which he's stoking with wood to generate heat to cook pizza. He's tall, wears only shorts, has a long white beard and looks like a hyperactive version of Gandalf the Magician.

The oven works well enough and soon we're tucking into delicious home-made pizza. It's a little crunchy, where fragments of charcoal from the burning wood have landed on the tomato sauce topping, but definitely eatable.

The full moon shines down on us and, in spite of the absence of deafening trance music, we all enjoy the evening.

Pune Diary 28

Goodbye to the beach

Slowly, slowly, I am getting ready to leave Goa. It's beautiful to wake up in the morning, go down to the sea and stroll along the beach while the sun comes up. It's beautiful to sit with friends in the evening and watch the sun sinking into the ocean, then go for a meal together.

These things feel good and the warm-hearted friendliness between sannyasins makes it easy to relax and enjoy a simple life. But I've never been a great one for lying on sunbeds all day, reading books and oiling my body.

I've been trying hard to get myself a tan. My face is brown and my body has acquired a kind of 'off-white' colour which, with my kind of skin, is as good as I can hope. But it will take many more weeks to get a real tan and this I'm not prepared to endure.

Besides, I have to face it: a hunger for meditation is creeping up on me. Some people tell me they can meditate in Goa, but it's not something that comes naturally to me. I need the support of a silent, buddhafield atmosphere, shared by many others, to persuade myself to look in.

I remember a story from the late 80s, soon after Osho returned to Pune, having come back from his world tour. One fine day, the Chief Minister and Finance Minister of Goa showed up at the resort, offering several acres of beachfront property for about the same price as a single mansion in Koregaon Park.

They were hoping, of course, that the Osho circus would

shift, lock-stock-and-barrel, to the beach, thereby attracting people and business to their state. The message went in to Osho and he replied, "Tell them 'no', because the energy at the beach is 'out' and asleep, and my work is 'in' and intense."

So that's how we missed meditating on the beach. But I can see his point. I love Goa and I love the feeling of relaxation and physical well-being that comes to me here. But I need to balance the inner and outer, so after 2-3 weeks I feel pulled to return to Pune, joining other meditators in the Evening Meeting in the Osho Auditorium.

It's a precious space and I have no idea how much longer it will be available, or, indeed, how much longer I will be free to come to India as I please. Life is mysterious, insecure, uncertain. What seems easy today may be impossible tomorrow.

So when Friday comes around, I'll be heading to Dabolim Airport and boarding Air India, on my way back to the place I've been visiting for the past 37 years. Time to spend a little more time exploring that inner space which seems so familiar and yet still unknown.

Pune Diary 29

Pune's purple haze

"This is your captain speaking. We are approaching Pune. Our altitude is approximately 3000 metres. If you look out your window, you will see a thick purple haze in the sky surrounding us, filling in the gaps between the white clouds. This is atmospheric pollution generated by the city beneath us. Thank you for flying Air India."

Well, actually, our pilot didn't say that. But he could have. I don't know if Jimi Hendrix was inspired by a similar situation when he wrote his classic 'Purple Haze',

or if Prince was alluding to the same phenomenon in his mega-hit ballad 'Purple Rain'.

But anyway, the truth is, Pune shrouds itself in a purple dome of ozone. Coming in from Goa's coastal beaches, which are relatively pollution free – well, the air is clean, if not the ground – was quite a paradigm shift.

Looking down at the city as we approached the airport, Pune seemed shrouded in man-made mist. But a few minutes later, stepping out of the plane and taking a few cautious breaths, the air didn't seem too bad. I could breathe okay and didn't immediately start coughing, although I have to admit it was nice to ride to Koregaon Park in an air-conditioned car.

My taxi driver was late for another job, so he dropped me rather hastily in Lane Six where I was obliged to transfer to a rickshaw. This, I took as a gentle but firm reminder of the reality of daily life – from now on, I wouldn't be cruising around Pune in AC limos.

Looking at the canopy of huge trees that make Koregaon Park beautiful, I noticed with disappointment that their leaves were covered with dust and dirt. "Of course," I said to myself, with resignation, "This is what happens in the dry season... all the colours disappear under the dust."

Then, something odd happened: it began to rain! It was almost as if nature heard my remark and felt offended. By the time I paid off the rickshaw driver and carried my suitcase up to my room, it was pouring down and soon the leaves of all the trees, shrubs and plants outside my window were gleaming and green. For the end of January, six months away from the monsoon, this was indeed a miracle.

Next morning, walking around the block to the resort's

main gate, the sun was shining, the air fresh and cool, the lanes damp and clean, although the street sweepers were doing their very best to create some reassuring clouds of dust by swishing at fallen leaves with their long-handled brooms.

My old friend Krishna Prem was on the gate, announcing my return with "Hey everybody, look who's back from the beach!"

My pass was still valid, I bought a new sticker... in I went. It was only 9:30 am, but dance music was playing in the Multiversity Plaza, pulling me there to see crowds of people, all in maroon robes, boogying together and sorting themselves into groups:

Sudhir and Maneesha took 30 people into their workshop *Squeeze the Juice From Life*, Devendra and Anil took about 15 participants each into their groups, and Meera already had god-knows how many people in Buddha Grove in her painting training.

In short, the place was buzzing. Numbers had been down in December, leaving me wondering whether there would be a 'high season' this winter, but they bounced up in January... swings and roundabouts... highs and lows...

The resort, as many sannyasins know, is surrounded by controversy, with legal struggles over trademarks, property transfers, copyright and all kinds of issues about who are the rightful heirs to Osho's legacy. Fortunately, these occur on another plane of existence. What I mean is: when you walk in the gate, you don't see them. They remain invisible to those of us who wish to enjoy the meditative atmosphere, aesthetic surroundings and opportunity to meet friends.

And even though I'm determined to be an innocent bystander amid the politics and power struggles, I have to say that, for now, for this one brief shining moment, for this sunny morning in late January – judging by the happy crowd in the Plaza – this place is alive, well and dancing.

Pune Diary 30

Forex dealings and migraine attacks

"Rate is good for euro... Swiss franc also..."

My forex dealer is consulting his smartphone. Whatever the rate, I will take what he offers. I really can't be bothered to walk around all the dealers in Koregaon Park comparing prices.

I used to do that, when I was bonded in loyalty to the forex guy in Lane One, who cohabits a ramshackle, tent-like shop with a woman who sells robes, clothes, shoes and coconuts. His financial supplier never gave him good rates. I had to go to other dealers, find the best rate, go back to him, tell him the rate, wait for him to call his supplier and get approval... Only then was he able to pay me the higher rate.

Eventually, I just started walking past him and after a few tries he stopped asking if I wanted to change money. The look of wounded betrayal on his face said it all. He knew I'd abandoned him.

Today's deal is done. I have changed 1000 Swiss francs and 500 euro, getting 111,000 rupees in return, which, even in bundles of 1000-rupee notes, amounts to a pretty thick wad.

When I first came to India, back in '76, there was no euro and I had no clue about the value of Swiss Francs. But I do recall getting 18 rupees to the pound sterling. Now I would get 80.

Coming out of this little shop, my jeans are stuffed

with swollen envelopes of rupees. I feel nervous, like I'm a walking invitation for a mugging, but maybe my supplier has protection on this street because so far nothing has ever happened.

Nevertheless, stepping into a rickshaw feels good and in a couple of minutes I'm back at my apartment and unloading the first envelope: 20,000 in rent to my landlady for the month of February.

Changing into a maroon robe, I stuff the rest of the money into my pockets and walk along the backstreets of Koregaon Park feeling a little absurd... the envelopes give me wide, protruding hips, like a fat woman in an oversized sari.

Again, I'm feeling uncomfortably like a mugger's dream come true, but nothing happens, even though there are 250 million people who go to bed hungry every night in

India and I'm carrying enough money to feed a poor family for five years. Such is the acceptance of wealth disparity in India.

I enter the resort's back gate, making my way along a winding path to Buddha Grove, where a friend of mine from Denmark is participating in Meera's painting training.

I see her immediately. She is lying prostrate on the ground, face down, arms outstretched, on top of a huge blank sheet of white art paper, as if in silent prayer. She desperately needs an additional 50,000 rupees to complete the training.

"Your prayers have been answered," I whisper, gently slipping a fat envelope under her hand. Payback time is set for two weeks.

A few moments later, I'm in the welcome centre, buying a month-long pass for 24,000 INR – a big saving over the daily rate – and realize to my astonishment that within a few minutes almost all the money has gone. Just a few rupees left for coconuts, rice, dhal and cappuccino.

I'm not even sure I want to stay here a month, but I hate buying a daily sticker and somehow have a strong desire to feel I'm *really here*. An eternal tourist like me has to put his roots down somewhere, even if it's only for a month.

All these financial goings on are way too much for my poor head, which soon develops a full-on migraine. I'm convinced I have a brain tumour but it may just be caffeine withdrawal or an overdose of peering into laptop screens. Time to go home and back to bed.

But the migraine just gets worse. Paracetamol doesn't work and at its height the throbbing ache inside my skull makes it too painful to lie down, sit, or stand up... all options blocked and my head is splitting apart. In despair,

I start weeping piteously, feeling extremely sorry for myself, like some five year-old whose mother just got run over by a truck... and force myself to throw up in the toilet.

Life in India is like this. Illnesses and upsets come with sudden ferocity, without warning. The status of your personal health and welfare barometer can swing from 'okay' to 'nearly fatal' in minutes.

However, these two gestures, weeping and throwing up, bring some relief. At least I can lie down now... and yes... soon fall asleep. Ah, oblivion, how I love thee!

Waking up two hours later, pain free, I notice with pleasant surprise that my mind is completely blank, filled exclusively with white, fluffy, cotton wool – soft, clean and virgin.

I go to the toilet in a state of No Mind, then find myself wondering "So this is how Osho walked to the bathroom?" Amazing!

For the next two hours I watch my mind trying to regain control of my head and when it finally succeeds I reach for the laptop:

Aummmmmmmmmmm...

Pune Diary 31

Magic show baba?

The magicians are having a hard time. At least, that's what they tell me. It's Saturday evening on the back gate lane, behind the resort, and four of them are squatting by the roadside at the junction where the road to Osho Teerth Park begins.

This is a good spot for business. In earlier times, when sannyasins were more numerous, a smartly-dressed man stood here every day selling fruit from a trolley at outrageous prices, guessing correctly that Westerners would pay up rather than make the effort to go shopping.

I used to buy freshly sliced pineapple from him until one day I saw him emerging from the bushes while pulling up his trousers. With no wash basin in sight, I decided the health risk was too great and put the pineapple snacks on hold.

Nowadays, these magicians cater to a different clientele. It's mainly families from India's emerging middle class who come to visit the park on weekends, offering business opportunities for these craftsmen of illusion.

Each magician has his small cloth bag of tricks and two of them are holding a twig of leaves, the easiest way to catch people.

"Hello madam, hello sir, kindly smell this leaf..."

As you hold the twig, they ask you to think of the scent from your favourite flower, which usually turns out to be a rose or a lotus. Meanwhile, an invisible paste containing perfumes from five popular flowers has been smeared on your hand, without you even noticing.

Naturally, when you lean close to smell the leaves, you get a whiff. Presto! Pure magic and a seductive introduction to the main event.

"Now come sir, see magic show... come this side... sit down... just five minutes... very good show, sir!"

These days, they leave me alone, apart from a nodded greeting, which I take as some kind of respect, since they no longer regard me as a tourist, just part of the local scenery. But today one of them approaches me: "Sir, I had no food today, eating only fruit... business very bad..." He looks suitably sad, but not really hungry and certainly not thin.

Another one takes up the theme: "Please tell us our

mistake, sir, what we have done wrong. To be without means to support ourselves..."

I smile at them good naturedly and namaste in a friendly way, but my rupees stay in my pocket. Once, I made the mistake of paying them 200 rupees to teach me a trick and after that they never left me alone for months, offering to teach me an entire magic show for ridiculous sums of money. So much for guarding the secrets of their trade.

Two of them used to get money from me quite regularly, but both are gone. One was a very old man, fragile and thin as a rake, with a long white beard, who looked like a cousin of Ho Chi Minh, Vietnam's legendary leader in the war against the United States.

This old magician was adopted by several sannyasins and toward the end of his life got money from us just for showing up on the street. He was too frail to do magic.

The other was his nephew, a tall fellow with dark hair, big brown eyes and a mournful face who somehow managed to persuade me to give him 200 rupees every year during Diwali.

Both have departed for the Great Magic Show in the Sky.

Meanwhile, inside the resort, in the dining area, another show is under way. A black-faced, silver-coloured monkey is sitting in a tree by the waterfall. The crows are indignant and noisily protesting, cawing at him like crazy, because this is their territory. They virtually own the bamboo grove next to the waterfall and even succeed in driving off big hawks when they try to nest in a nearby tree.

Suddenly, the monkey jumps to the ground and, leaping from table to table in spectacular fashion – he'd easily win the long jump in the Olympics – is quickly on the other side of the dining area. His antics stop scores of dining sannyasins in mid-mouthful and quickly draw a crowd.

"No photography in the resort!" yells a voice, but the mobile phones are out and the cameras are clicking as maroon-robed humans track their distant cousin's travels. I guess he's hoping for a stray banana, so maybe my little snack is safe – it's Saturday and that means chocolate brownies for tea in Meera Canteen.

Do monkeys eat brownies? I hope I'll never find out.

P.S. By the way, just to clarify: I talk about two Meeras in these diaries. One is the resort's canteen. The other is my friend, the Japanese artist. In case you're wondering, the canteen isn't named after my friend. Both are named after the Indian female saint, Meera, whose songs of devotion to Krishna are still popular and revered throughout India.

Pune Diary 32

Self portrait at soul depth

I guess I'm a morning person. I like walking the lanes of Koregaon Park as the sun peeps over the mansions and shafts of yellow light start filtering softly through the trees, creating pillars of light. The effect is enchanting and mystical. I almost expect Captain Kirk of the starship Enterprise to step into one of them and utter his immortal line "Beam me up, Scotty."

My aim is to arrive at the resort's back gate around 8:00 am, looking forward to a breakfast of banana porridge, happy to be inside the magic bubble before the traffic gets serious.

Passing through the resort's Plaza area, I see the hired staff are busy cleaning up from last night's show when Meera, the Japanese painter, and her 35 group participants staged a colourful extravaganza - no other word for it - of dance and theatre and delight.

Meera's shows always verge on the edge of chaos because they are barely rehearsed, but there's such a spirit of fun and vitality among her group that nobody cares... least of all the audience.

It's lovely to watch so many people dancing together and feel how bonded and carefree they've become during the 25 days of Meera's painting training... pure delight.

The training is now over and Buddha Grove is surrounded by their creations, hanging in colourful splashes of colour from nylon ropes tied between the trees.

The 'primal paintings' are abstract and chaotic – bound to be so, because the main lesson Meera teaches in this section is to abandon form and structure in favour of spontaneous feeling and flow.

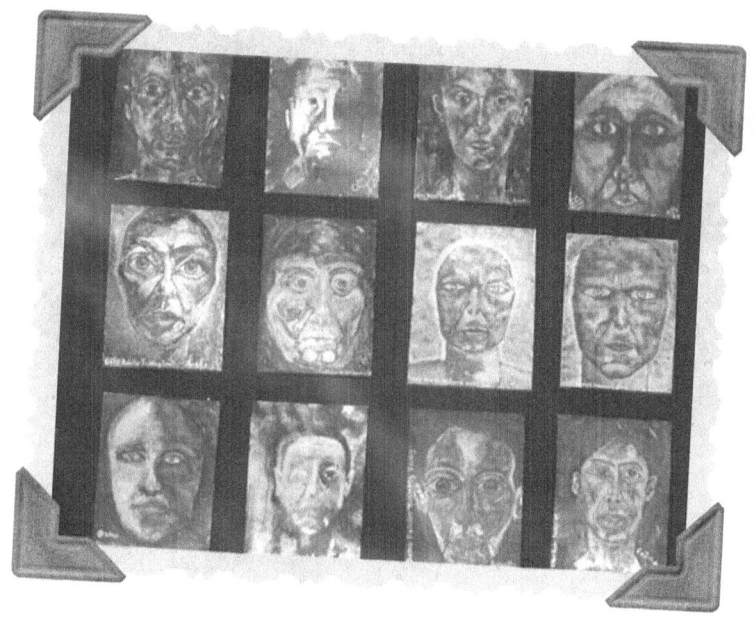

The 'nature paintings' are a million different shades of green, vividly portraying the dense foliage surrounding Buddha Grove, offering labyrinths of interwoven branches and leaves. Some are truly beautiful.

But the exhibit with most impact is the long row of self-portraits, standing on the marble floor of Buddha Grove, placed in a line around the old podium where Osho used to speak. These are austerely painted in black, white and grey. Their unsmiling, intense faces stare at you from the depths of their souls, showing how deeply the painters have been looking at themselves – not a single superficial smile to be seen.

Scary stuff. In fact, one of the teachers of a morning class in the 'Grove felt compelled to turn the portraits around so they wouldn't distract and disturb her participants, so magnetic and provocative is their power.

Meera, by the way, is also a walking pharmacy, always on the lookout for people like myself with colds, so she can administer her potions... "No, wait!" she says, as I walk by, sniffing into a tissue. "Vitamin C! Here, from the West... very good quality... and this... from Japan, very expensive, take one... you want noodles tonight?"

It is an awesome aspect of Meera's energy and compassion that she can deliver hot noodles to your door on her scooter while taking care of a big painting training.

This time, though, I rescue myself with a *neti pot*... the ancient yogic art of pouring warm salt water into one nostril of your nose until it floods your sinuses and pours out the other nostril – you hold your head sideways for this, by the way.

It didn't stop the cold, but performed the crucial function of keeping my nose clear and preventing mucus from getting down into my chest. No cough. So Evening Meeting is okay for this not-so-sick swami.

We gather in our white robes at nightfall, waiting patiently across the water from the auditorium. It's one of my favourite moments of the day. Changing into white and leaving everything behind in my locker somehow signals a break from ordinary life, an invitation to drop it all and turn inward.

"Open!" says an authoritative voice behind us, where the security check is performed. Off we go, across the water, walking together along the narrow, spiritual catwalk towards the pyramid, one long flowing river of white.

"Stop! Stop!"

A figure suddenly appears above us, in the doorway of the pyramid, at the top of the steps. "You can't go in yet... there's an audio problem." Our procession halts, temporarily confused by conflicting commands.

But from behind, the authoritative voice from the security check shouts "Go! Go!"

In my experience, when faced with 'stop' and 'go' together, it's usually more fun to go, so I walk up the steps and others follow. As we come into the auditorium, the guys on the mixing board look at us in surprise, the sound-check for the musicians is hastily finished and the huge mixer is rolled away across the marble floor.

No problem. The band begins to play, music is happening and we dance to shake off the day before sitting silently in meditation.

Tonight's gem from Osho: "With a teacher you are taught... with a Master you are caught."

He got that right.

Pune Diary 33

Old hangout

It's not the same. Well, of course, it wouldn't be. The old-style German Bakery disappeared four years ago, on February 13, 2010, when a terrorist bomb exploded, killing 17 people and injuring 60 more. It never came back. It never resurrected.

The new German Bakery is on the same site, but it's not a recognizable reincarnation. It's a totally different creature. It's too clean. It's too tidy. It's too straight. It's way too middle class.

You enter through a metal detector and security check and come into a light, airy coffee shop, with a white-painted fence surrounding the L-shaped layout, shielding it from the traffic outside.

There's only one entrance now, not two – part of the security that was missing four years ago when they really needed it. The bakery sells coffee and chai, plus a host of cookies and cakes, some of which are reminiscent of bygone days.

But the whole vibe has changed. It's no longer that crowded, chaotic mix of hippies, sannyasins, local hustlers and newly-arrived tourists... all rubbing shoulders, sharing wooden tables, sitting on stools, eating salads and veggie burgers, drinking fresh-squeezed juices and barley coffee, reading newspapers and consulting the Lonely Planet Guide to India.

The bomb that destroyed the bakery had been left in a

backpack filled with RDX explosives under a table, planted there – so the police say – by the Indian *mujahedeen* Islamic group, working with other terrorist organizations who instigated the 2008 attack against the Taj Hotel and other targets in Mumbai.

The bomb was either on a timer, or meant to be triggered by a signal from a mobile phone. Either way, it had been lying under the table for quite a long time, until around 7:15 pm, when customers pointed it out to the staff and a waiter grabbed hold of it and started to drag it out. Only then did the explosion happen.

So maybe there was a fault in the trigger mechanism, delaying the blast, which proved to be a lifesaver for sannyasins, many of whom had – by that time – left to go to the Evening Meeting or to attend a local concert by a well-known musician.

On that particular day, I was tired and had decided not to go to the Evening Meeting. So I was lying on my bed, in my room on Lane 2, when I heard it. The building shook. "That's a bomb," I thought. The feeling is unmistakeable. I reached for the phone and dialled the resort's main gate.

"Was that you?" I asked, anxiously.

"No, further over, towards North Main Road," the guard replied.

A few minutes later, a local man arrived at our bungalow on his bicycle, bringing news that a gas cylinder had exploded in the German Bakery's kitchen.

"What nonsense," I thought. No ordinary gas cylinder could make a sound like that. Sure enough, a little while later, the real story emerged: it was a bomb.

Later that same evening, the Plaza in the resort was crowded with sannyasins and visitors. Somehow, we all felt the need to come together, connect with each other, feeling a shared, unspoken gratitude that we were safe.

Not everyone came. One Italian woman died in the blast and several Indian sannyasins were either dead or injured. Still, there was a feeling of relief – there could have been so many more casualties.

The aim of the perpetrators was to cause shock waves around the world and tarnish India's reputation as a safe destination for foreigners, but this time it didn't really work. There weren't enough deaths to cause much of a ripple in the international media.

But we certainly noticed the fall-out in Koregaon Park: massive police security and tighter controls at the resort's entrances, including airport-style scanning machines for bags. We also learned that both the bakery and the resort had been visited by David Headley, an American-Pakistani intelligence officer working for terrorist organizations, who had toured India compiling a list of 'soft targets'.

For several years after the explosion, the bakery stood as a ruin, looking forlorn and desolate, while compensation claims were pursued and arguments dragged on between the owners and the staff. Now, at last, it's open again.

Today, for old time's sake, I make a visit, but am prevented from taking video clips with my iPhone. "No photography outside," caution the security guards. My bag is inspected and I'm asked to leave my water bottle behind. Then I can walk through the metal detector and into the bakery.

The pretty young woman behind the counter is wearing a protective cap over her hair and plastic gloves for hygienic food handling. Hmm... that's certainly different than before the blast.

The cookies and cakes look good, so I buy myself a slice of apple pie – my old favourite – but have no feeling to stay. For better or worse, this part of my life, of many of our lives, is over. In a way, it's no big deal. I never went there much, anyway, and the widening of North Main Road – conducted by Pune Corporation a few years earlier – had already damaged the original ambience.

But it was somehow comforting to have it there, like a cosy spot in my mind, reminding me I had a place to go when nothing else would satisfy me except a barley coffee and a slice of apple pie.

I'm not one for nostalgia. But I miss it.

Pune Diary 34

New hangout

Having paid my respects to the passing of an era, I head down German Bakery Lane to the Yogi Tree Restaurant. This place also changed with the bakery blast. It used to be located under the Hotel Surya Villa, but the Pune police came under intense political pressure to enforce strict regulations on all street-side cafés and restaurants, so for a while it was shut down.

With both the bakery and the Yogi Tree gone, eating out in Koregaon Park became a dismal affair. Prems still served decent Indian food, but was largely taken over by young, trendy, middle class Puneites. Next to the resort, Dario's Italian cuisine flourished, but it was a real restaurant – rapidly becoming fashionable with Pune's *nouveau riche* – and didn't really qualify as a casual hang out spot for sannyasins.

The Yogi Tree was able to combine a relaxed atmosphere with great food, including brown rice, tofu steaks, fresh greens and other healthy stuff. It was a godsend when I was sick and served the best ginger-lemon-honey tea for miles around.

Slowly, as the iron grip of police regulations relaxed, an alternative site for the Yogi Tree opened up next door to the hotel, in a wide, sunken space just off German Bakery Lane. The new site was outdoors, cool in the morning and evening, but blazing hot in the midday sun, discouraging customers until the managers finally understood the need for large sunshades over the tables.

This afternoon, I arrive to discover that my friend Savita has occupied half the restaurant to stage a launching party for her book about Osho, titled *Encounters with an Inexplicable Man*. It's the end product of five long years of hard work, during which she interviewed over 40 people from 12 different countries to gather 95 personal stories about incidents with our favourite mystic.

It was Savita who inspired me to write my own book, *My Dance with a Madman*. When she asked me for a short anecdote to put in her book, I quickly wrote three and sent them to her. It was fun and easy. I'm a journalist by trade and can write short stories standing on my head, blindfold and whistling Dixie – well, you know what I mean. It's not difficult.

"Very nice," said Savita, after reading them, "But I'm only going to use one."

That didn't feel right. I liked those stories and wanted people to read all three. Then I realized: if writing short anecdotes came so easily to me, why not just keep writing them and publish my own book?

I'd known, as soon as Osho died, that I wanted to write a book about my life with him, but for 20 years I'd hesitated, because I couldn't think of a suitable format. A day-by-day chronology seemed boring, yet I had interesting tales to tell.

Now, suddenly, here was the key to unlock my treasure chest of memories: a book of short anecdotes, loosely tied together in some kind of chronological order, giving vivid snapshots of my life with 'Big B'.

After two decades of waiting, a book of 60 anecdotes popped out of me in six months, just like an overdue baby. Thank you, Savita, for the inspiration.

The Yogi Tree is full of people. At one end of the restaurant, a pile of books stands on a table and two friends are busy selling while Savita sits at an adjoining table, signing copies.

My story got dropped by the way, because she'd collected far too many anecdotes and mine had already been published in my own book. But, to my surprise and delight, I see that I wrote the 'Foreword', a contribution which I'd entirely forgotten.

It begins: "What did Mary Magdalene really say to Jesus? What if Judas had written anecdotes about his years with his master...?"

You get the point. I'm saying that Savita's book is important because all these personal recollections of moments with Osho offer a unique perspective on how he inter-acted with the world in all kinds of situations – like talking with an auto dealer in New Jersey, for example, or hypnotizing a dog (I kid you not).

The event is a great success. Lots of people show up, Savita is happy, many books are sold, the chai is free and the cheesecake is delicious. With a bit of luck, I'll just make it back to the resort in time for the Evening Meeting.

Pune Diary 35

Are you still rebellious?

I'm sitting on a low wall, close to the two little lakes in front of Osho Auditorium, waiting in my white robe for the Evening Meeting. A studious-looking man of about 70, also in white, comes and sits on the wall beside me.

"You are Anand Sutubi?" he asks, quietly.

"Subhuti," I correct him.

He smiles. "I just read your book, *My Dance with a Madman* – very inspiring," he tells me.

"Thank you."

There is a pause, then he asks me, in a thoughtful kind of way, "Tell me... are you still rebellious?"

Whoa. There's a question I haven't heard before, at least, not posed like that. It takes me by surprise and I have to think about it.

"Well... hmm... if rebelliousness is trying to move beyond my conditioning, then I guess what's challenging me right now are my sexual attitudes," I tell him.

Then I explain: how my body and my energy are perfectly content for nothing much to happen in the way of love affairs and love-making, while my mind insists that unless something does happen I'm losing my identity as a man.

Normally, at this point in life, a traditional sannyasin might, as Osho puts it, "turn his face towards the forest" and leave behind all worldly concerns, heading for a cave in the Himalayas.

Here in Pune, though, it's rather different. There's no

escape from life's challenges.

It so happens that two friends of mine, both young Indian guys who married Western women and went to the 'First World' to seek fame and fortune, returned recently – both single once more – and we've been hanging out together.

One is extremely good-looking, while the other has a funny, loveable way with women that seems irresistible. So I'm surrounded by a whirlwind of flirting, dating and sexual encounters, which is enjoyable and full of laughter and fun.

However, there's a *Catch 22* in this dance. It swirls around me, but it doesn't involve me. The boys are dating. The girls are lovely. I'm included in the daytime games but not in the night-time pleasures.

That's the challenge: to see, feel and touch this familiar space while understanding and accepting that it's no longer my story. Romantic stirrings do occur, from time to time, but with long breaks in between – nothing like the full-on dating game that is unfolding around me.

My only romantic stirrings in recent weeks were triggered by a Russian woman who, fortunately or unfortunately, left for Moscow before anything could begin.

"Of course, you never know about tomorrow," I add cautiously, as I explain the situation to the man beside me.

He listens attentively and I think I'm impressing him with my candid and profound confession, but it turns out he's on a totally different track. "I mean rebelling against the system," he informs me, and explains that he is a psychiatric nurse in Belgium, trying to bring new and more humanitarian ideas into his working life.

"Are you still rebellious in this way?" he persists.

"The system? I never really engage it," I reply. "It's something that supplies me with a credit card, a passport and a small pension... and that's about it."

And there we have to leave our conversation, as the white-robed people around us are given the green light and start to cross the waters, heading for the auditorium.

After the Evening Meeting and dinner, I wander into Buddha Grove where rows of meditation cushions have been set out for the Full Moon Meditation. Wisely, this is held a couple of days ahead of the actual full moon, since this allows the shining, silvery orb to be much higher in the sky than it would otherwise be.

The lights are turned off, musicians begin to play soft music from their perch on the podium, and the white marble floor glows with a silvery light, reflected from the sky above us. Maybe it's just me, but the moonlight in India seems different than in other countries. It's more mystical. It seems gentle, but over time it has a strength and penetrating power, so that when I close my eyes it's as if the moon is shining inside me as well.

The night-time temperature now is just perfect for this kind of thing, not too cold and not too hot, although, as we all know, as the hot season approaches it's going to get much, much warmer.

"Are you still rebellious?" The questions circles in my brain. Years ago, back in the 70s, I wore an orange suit to my job as a political reporter in the Houses of Parliament and made them call me 'Anand Subhuti'.

Then I joined Osho's circus and did battle with the mainstream by pumping out press releases about what he was saying – 'The pill is the greatest invention since the bullock cart' is one that will be forever imprinted on my mind.

But times change. These days, I don't go out of my way to fight the mainstream. Instead, I focus on getting the mainstream out of my head. That's an ongoing rebellion, for sure... and maybe it's enough.

Pune Diary 36

Okay gecko, go!

I like geckos. It's amusing to sit on a garden patio in Koregaon Park, on a warm summer's night, and watch these little lizards clinging to the wall of a house, close to an outdoor lamp, catching insects as they fly around, attracted by the light.

Sometimes, too, you see geckos sitting on the globe of the lamp itself, silhouetted by white or yellow light, looking like some kind of artistic decoration.

But I don't like geckos up close and personal. So, when I entered my room last night and switched on the light, I was annoyed to see a large, fat gecko squatting on the marble floor. For a moment, we locked eyeballs, staring at each other, then he quickly scooted under my bed.

Kneeling down and shining my flashlight into the darkness, I couldn't see him, which probably meant he was hiding in the tiny gap between the bed and the wall, right behind my pillow. Hmm... don't fancy trying to sleep with a gecko that close to my head.

Now, I'm a fairly tolerant guy and accept that in India you need to get along with all kinds of domesticated and undomesticated creatures. And, of course, if you live in a big room with a high ceiling you're going to have geckos and there's nothing you can do about it. And some people just *love* them.

But still, if I have a choice, I opt for a gecko-free environment. It's not that they're going to do me harm, although I did have one drop on my head once – he fell off the top of a door as I opened it. For a moment, we were both startled, then his razor-sharp claws scratched my skin as he scrambled over my head and neck, looking for a way off the human mountain onto which he'd fallen.

Those claws, by the way, are not for fighting. They need to be that sharp, so geckos can run upside down on ceilings, chasing insects. The tiny points of their nails can grip on almost nothing.

Still, that didn't lessen the shock when the little wannabe-dragon fell off my door and onto me. I tried to brush him off my head with my hand, but then he jumped onto my

hand and clung to it, until finally I was able to shake him loose, onto the floor, and he raced off.

That was years ago. Now I have to deal with this one. I

pulled the bed away from the wall and sure enough, there he was, looking bright-eyed and innocent, frozen to the wall. A few threatening hand gestures got him moving and my intention was to drive him under the door and out into the hall, but instead he hid behind my book shelf. No use trying to get him out of there.

I gave up and went to bed, making sure my mosquito net was firmly tucked in all the way around. I slept long and uneventfully.

Next morning, as the sun rose, I slid out of bed and pulled back my curtains to greet the day. Suddenly, the gecko popped out from under the curtain rail, freezing motionless on the wall at head height, a few centimetres away from me.

For a long moment, we stared at each other, eyeball-to-eyeball.

Slowly, so as not to frighten him, I backed off, then walked to the balcony door and opened it. Then, picking up my electric, mosquito-killing tennis racket, I tried to shift him gently towards the exit. I wasn't going to zap him, just herd him.

But he didn't move, even though the racket was inches from his nose.

As a survival strategy, it was an impressive exercise in denial. What he was saying to me was, "Hey, what are you looking at? I'm not here." But, of course, we both knew different.

I tapped the wall in front of him several times with the racket, coming closer and closer to his nose. Eventually, he got the message, turned around and scooted a few inches in the direction of the open door, before freezing again.

More tapping... more scooting... more tapping... more

scooting... and then at last he curled his body around the door post and was gone.

Thank you. Enjoy the great outdoors. Lots of insects out there, buddy. No need to hurry back.

Pune Diary 37

Is it enough now?

Once in a while, song lyrics hit me at exactly the right time and become awesomely profound. In a sense, it's nothing new. Casual and unintended listening has provoked deep self-reflection many times down the centuries.

For example, there's a famous story in Buddhist literature, relating how an ordinary citizen became enlightened, just because he happened to be passing a Buddhist monk who

was reciting the *Vajracchedika Prajnaparamita* verses of Gautam Siddhartha, also known as the *Diamond Sutra*.

The monk was not an awakened being, but his daily routine of reciting the Buddha's words provoked a sudden awakening, unintentionally, in a casual passer-by.

On a more modest scale, it was kinda like that this morning. I'd never heard of a pop group called *Xploding Plastix*, but I was dancing in Buddha Grove to music played by a new DJ, a young American guy who'd not been in the resort very long. All of a sudden, he started playing a number called *Sunset Spirals*.

The beat was light and catchy. At first, the lyrics meant nothing... something about landing at Heathrow Airport and seeing a friend wave a greeting. But then the chorus kicked in:

Is it enough now?
Is it enough now?
Is it enough now?

This morning, Buddha Grove was at its best. The sun was shining through the trees, it was a warm day and each little gust of a fresh breeze sent showers of dried bamboo leaves fluttering through the air, cascading gently all around us. A lovely woman came and hugged me, friends were saying 'hello' and dancing with me and there was nothing special on my mind.

Is it enough now...
Is this not enough now?

Who would have thought that a Norwegian electrofunk band could nail the essence of being here-and-now so neatly?

Because their simple lyrics opened a window and I found myself looking back on my life with a sense of wonder, seeing how much I have been driven by the hunger of discontent, by the chronic craving of never being satisfied, always wanting more... more money, more love, more success...

And here, on this sunny morning, for a few moments, it all fell away because there was an unexpected feeling of happiness and contentment in my heart and I could not deny the truth of those words pumping out through the sound system:

Is this not enough now?

It's funny, so many times I've heard Gautam Buddha say that the root of misery is desire, but this morning, maybe for the first time, I saw that for 68 years I've been running after 'more' and rarely pausing long enough to open my arms and welcome 'enough'.

Thank you, everyone, who danced with me this morning.

And as one friend pointed out: back in the 70s, when Osho was ending every discourse with those softly spoken words 'Enough for today', maybe he was waiting for us to nod and say 'Yes, today is enough unto itself, thank you'.

Speaking of the *Diamond Sutra*, it's a fascinating dialogue between Buddha and one of his disciples, the original Subhuti.

Buddha begins each sutra: *What do you think, Subhuti...* and then asks a really esoteric question, like... *Can it be said that a Buddha has 32 marks?* This is a reference to spiritual folk lore in India that enlightened beings share 32 similar physical characteristics, like long ear lobes, for example.

And Subhuti says something like: *No Lord, truly a Buddha has 32 no-marks, therefore only he can be said to have 32 marks...* mind-blowing stuff like this.

So when, in 1977, Osho was speaking on the *Diamond*

Sutra, I asked him a question: "What do you think, Bhagwan? Do I have the slightest idea what you're talking about, or would the slightest idea be the wrong thing to have?"

He answered 'Yes, Subhuti' – and went on to the next question! Leaving me nonplussed, with several wires fused in my brain.

Returning to the present: It's that time of year when the winter months are ending, the hot season is approaching, and people are on the move. The air in Koregaon Park is filled with travel plans.

Some are heading North to Rishikesh for yoga retreats and satsang offerings... others return from Goa and Hampi to stay for a few days before heading back to Europe... a big group of Lithuanians passes through on an all-India spiritual tour... and in a few days' time we can expect a new influx of people here as the high season ends and the off-season prices kick in.

Me? I have one more month to travel in India, so I expect that soon I'll be going somewhere. I just don't know where or when, so I'll hang out in Pune a bit longer and see which way the wind blows.

And maybe, once in a while, I'll pause amid all my daily doings and reflect on the spiritual mysticism hidden in the lyrics of an electro-funk hit...

Is it enough now?

Pune Diary 38

Neti pot nightmare

I should know by now: never take myself seriously at 3:30 in the morning. It's a time when common sense and perspective weaken, when imagined love affairs seem real and medical ailments grow out of all proportion.

How it happened: I came back to Pune from Goa and immediately caught a cold. Since I'd gone to Goa in the first place to get rid of a cough, this was unacceptable. I was determined to prevent it from going down into my throat and chest like last time.

That's when I picked up my *neti* pot and started flushing my nose three or four times a day. I figured that if I could

prevent a build-up of mucus, the infection wouldn't spread.

It worked. I still had the cold, but I could breathe easily and my throat and chest stayed healthy.

By the way, for the uninitiated, a *neti* pot looks like a small watering can and has been used by Hindus practicing Ayurveda for millennia. These pots used to be ceramic. Now they're plastic and sold for 20 rupees at any Indian pharmacy.

At first, I used filtered water, which I boiled and allowed to cool before adding salt and irrigating my nostrils. Then I got lazy. I figured warm tap water would be okay and also a lot quicker.

Then I got a headache. A very strange headache. I can say with confidence that 95 percent of my headaches are caused by working too long on my computer. Thus, when I stop staring into a laptop screen, they disappear.

But this one was different. It felt heavy and kinda circular, like a crown fitting too tightly on a monarch's head. Not quite as severe as the headache received by Viserys, in *Game of Thrones*, when Khal Drogo gave him a 'crown' by pouring molten gold over his head, but similar and persistent.

Whether I worked at my computer or not, it stayed with me. I went to bed with my headache, slept for a few hours and woke up with it again at 3:30 am.

I figured I might be over-using the *neti* pot – too much salt in my sinuses, or something – so I went online and googled '*neti* pot health'.

That's when I saw it. That's when Google brought me the news: 'Neti Pot Deaths'. That's when I read the headline: 'Deaths from brain-eating amoeba linked to sinus remedy for colds'.

A brain-eating amoeba? For nearly forty years I've been acquainted with the hazards of amoebas in my guts – an intrinsic part of the Indian experience – but in my brain? Fascinated and alarmed, I investigated further.

It turned out that two Americans in Louisiana died after using warm tap water to flush their noses with *neti* pots. The water contained an amoeba called *Naegleria Fowleri* that lodges in the mucus membranes of your nose, eats its way up your olfactory nerve and chews your brain until you're dead.

No cure.

Er... excuse me? Can you run that by me again? Yes, that's right... no cure.

OMG. Maybe I've got *Naegleria Fowleri* up my nose. Maybe, even now, they're chewing their way up my smelling nerves, eagerly anticipating a blow-out feast when they reach the grey matter of my forebrain.

I suppose the most shocking aspect of such situations is the realization that it's already too late – that something which was done so easily, without a care in the world, could have irreversible and fatal consequences.

Quickly, I read on, hoping for the best, dreading the worst.

Bad news: *Naegleria Fowleri* like to live in warm climates.

More bad news: Symptoms include unusual headaches. Oh no!

Practical tip: The most reliable indicator of *Naegleria Fowleri* infection is that your sense of smell disappears. Well, naturally, if some hungry bug is eating away your olfactory nerve...

Reaching for the honey pot, I unscrewed the lid and

inhaled deeply. Mmmm... yes... definitely smells like honey. Same with eucalyptus oil. So far, so good.

My old friend Abhiyana, acupuncturist and former resident of the Pune ashram, was online at his home in Sedona, Arizona, so I told him my fears. He did his best to reassure me, sharing memories of Varanasi, where he saw sadhus sitting by the Ganges, flushing their noses daily with *neti* pots filled with river water.

Maybe *Naegleria Fowleri* don't live in India. If they do, maybe they can't survive Pune Corporation's water treatment plants. If they can, maybe they don't like my nose. Maybe, after all, I will see the dawn.

I relaxed and made myself a cup of tea, opening the door to the balcony. A familiar wave of sewage odour filled the room as Pune Corporation performed its regular habit of dumping untreated human waste into the Mula-Mutha River.

Aaaah... yes... that smells soooooo good!

Pune Diary 39

The ultimate test

My old friend Nisarg, sitting with me at lunch in Meera Canteen, insists that I write about stool tests. "People need to know, and you can make it funny," she tells me.

I'm not enthusiastic, especially while eating my delicious organic steamed veggies. But Anne, sitting with us, wants to know. Anne is in her twenties, from Norway, and has been travelling for two months in Goa, Hampi and Gokana. She has pains in her upper abdomen, which could be a sign that she has uninvited guests in her intestines.

Okay. Since I just wrote about brain-eating amoebas, I may as well shine a little light on the more common variety: those that hang out in the human digestive system, happily eating away our insides.

This amoeba is called *Entamoeba Hystolica* and is passed from human to human in the form of cysts, usually by infected people handling water, juices and food. They're very successful and popular – it's estimated that 500 million people worldwide play host to this this amoeba.

My golden rules for long term survival in India used to be: never drink water offered at restaurants, never drink fresh-squeezed juices anywhere, never eat uncooked food and carefully remove all garnish sprinkled as decoration on cooked food.

These days, I'm more relaxed. I eat avocado salads in Dario's, fruit muesli in the Yogi Tree and sip fresh juices at Pete's Shack in Goa. But still, I try to be careful.

Back in the 70s, we avoided water and instead drank bottled soda-water. That's how fresh-lime sodas became so popular among sannyasins – it was the closest thing to water we could risk drinking. These days, however, bottled mineral water is fine and the resort also provides free, filtered, good-quality drinking water for all visitors.

So, down to basics: 'stool test' is a polite term for 'shit test'. After wintering in India, I usually take one at the end of March, just before leaving, to check if my guts are okay. Sometimes I have symptoms, like gas, bloating, 'loose motion' (polite term for 'runny shit') and sometimes not. Anyway, I usually check.

I go to Hemotech Laboratories, the people who conduct the resort's AIDS tests. They have a lab just off Dhole Patil Road, opposite Ruby Hall Hospital, on a street called

'Chatrupati Shahi Maharaj Road' – try telling that to a rickshaw driver.

The lab at Inlaks Hospital is more convenient, being next to the resort, but in my experience useless. They never find anything in stool samples. Once, to prove my point, when I had amoebas, I took one test at Hemotech and another at Inlaks.

Hemotech found them. Inlaks didn't. So, if you want to pretend you don't have amoebas, Inlaks is definitely your best choice.

There's an art to providing a stool sample. At Hemotech, the lab technician starts around ten, so you want to take a shit as late as possible, no earlier than 9:00 am, so that it's nice and fresh. And you need the very last piece of shit to come out, because that's been furthest up your gut.

Best method: pass motion on a bunch of toilet paper and take the sample from there.

Oh, I forgot, before starting your 'motion', go to Krishna Medical pharmacy on North Main Road and buy a 'specimen container' – a small plastic jar with screw-on lid – and a small wooden spatula. Spoon the sample into the jar with the spatula, close the lid and you're done. Jump in a rickshaw and head for Hemotech.

A stool test costs a mere 150 rupees, less than a couple of quid, so you can do it every day for a month if you want to, without damaging your bank account. Usually, that's not necessary.

The great thing about Hemotech is they deliver the results to their AIDS-test man in the resort's welcome centre. You pick them up next day at 5:00 pm.

When you look at the results, the key words are: 'ent. hystolica'. This means you've got amoebas. Another key word is 'cysts'. This also means you've got amoebas, but in dormant form, so if you have no actual symptoms then treatment is optional. The presence of a few pus cells doesn't mean much, but if you have a lot of pus cells this could also indicate amoebas in action.

Best treatment: a five or ten-day course of flagyl-based antibiotics like *Tinidazole* and *Metronidazole* are effective cures, if you can stand the 'I'm poisoning myself' feeling of nausea that usually goes with it.

I usually opt for a short cut: a two-pill power-pack called *Secnal*, taken once only. Buy it at Krishna Medical but don't take it until you're out of India and safely home in Germany, or wherever you live. You don't want to risk reinfection and having to take another mega-dose.

Alternative cures include various Ayurvedic cleanses and potions which may or may not do the trick. Personally, if I'm sure I have amoebas I go for *Secnal*. If it's uncertain, I might experiment with alternatives first.

After consuming antibiotics, be sure to replenish your stomach's friendly bacteria with acidophilus. And like they say in drug commercials to avoid lawsuits: if symptoms persist, see a doctor.

Okay? Now, back to my lunch... bon appetit!

Pune Diary 40

The back gate brotherhood

We come and go. They stay. We need a ride somewhere. They take us.

Ever walked through the resort's back gate during the past 20 years? If so, chances are you rubbed shoulders with two guys who spend a lot of time there.

Their names are Shiva and Tanaji. Shiva is the younger of the two, has black hair and a moustache and almost always wears a white shirt. Tanaji goes by the nickname 'uncle'. He is older and less talkative, with a greying beard. It seems like his favourite colour is brown because mostly that's what he wears.

Their occupation? Shiva and Tanaji are two of our best-known neighbourhood rickshaw drivers. By inclination, they like to work only from the resort's back gate on Lane 2, but for practical, economic reasons that's not always possible.

"Low season is coming, so we have to go outside to find business," explains Shiva. "But we come here anyway... after lunch... for some time, every day."

Both men have been using Lane 2 as their centre of operations for more than two decades. Mobile phones have helped them stay connected with long term Western residents in the Koregaon Park area, who hire them to run errands: picking up laundry, making Xerox copies, ferrying groceries... any kind of job that needs a driver.

For me, the connection pays off when I have to make

a local trip involving two or three stops at different destinations. Then it's great to keep the same driver, rather than trying to flag down a different rickshaw after each stop. It probably works out more expensive – gotta keep our guys happy – but the convenience is worth it.

"Ever have an accident?" I asked Shiva as we waited for the traffic lights, where North Main Road intersects with the road to Yerawada Bridge.

"Yes, big one... in '94... I was drunk... my fault," he said, unashamedly. "I hit motorbike in Lane 2... rickshaw overturn on me..." he made a flipping motion with his hand. "Motorbike was okay, but I got hurt..." he pulled his shirt off his shoulder to reveal a scar. "After that, no more drinking."

And now, an unrelated rickshaw anecdote:

"Don't these things have doors?" asked an elegant, wealthy Russian woman, now living in Dubai, sitting beside me in a rickshaw as we charged madly through rush-hour traffic towards MG Road one evening. I shook my head.

"But what happens when it rains?" she wondered.

I pointed to a rolled up plastic sheet attached to the roof on her side of the rickshaw. "That comes down, on one side only. Keeping dry in a downpour is a real challenge."

She shook her head in disbelief.

And now, some rickshaw rules, learned the hard way:

Rickshaw drivers who are waiting in a line never go by meter. If you try to insist on 'meter fare' you will quickly become embroiled in a useless and frustrating argument, the only cure for which is screaming loudly in Dynamic Meditation in Osho Auditorium the following morning.

Accept the inevitable and negotiate. Warning: it is essential to fix the price of your trip before stepping into the rickshaw. Trying to bargain at your destination is like pulling a wad of notes out of your purse and saying "Here, how much do you want?"

Short local fares are now 20 rupees and even though the drivers ask for 30-50 rupees they will usually come down to the base rate, especially if they know you've been here awhile. Often, the final figure depends on how much time and energy you like to invest in bargaining, complaining, looking angry, looking bored and pretending to walk away.

The meter fare to MG Road is 50-60 rupees, but you will probably be asked 'Coming back, baba?' If you say 'no' then you may need to add another 30 because 'coming back empty... long way... no business.'

At night, of course you pay at least 50 percent more –

'night-time charges, baba' – although as far as I can tell the amount of fuel consumed by the rickshaw is the same in darkness as in daylight, so the reason for this nocturnal fare hike is something of a mystery.

Rickshaws that you flag down as they speed along North Main Road and other routes will usually go by meter. Many of these meters are now electronic and actually state the real fare, as opposed to the old, wind-up meters whose rates had to be multiplied by ten or more.

One final word from Shiva:

"If you make a report on us, say 'hello' to our customers!"

Will do.

Pune Diary 41

Freedom at midnight

"**You know, Subhuti, my three-month** visa expires at midnight on Thursday, but my flight is not until four-thirty on Friday morning, so I'll just check in early, go through immigration and wait in the transit area. I'll be fine."

"You can't check in that early."

"Okay, so I'll go through immigration control after midnight. I expect they'll just waive me through... after all, it's only a few hours."

"They won't let you go."

"They have to! Surely, there is a period of grace... a few hours...?"

"Nope."

"But what can they do?"

"They'll stop you. You'll miss your flight. They'll send you back to Pune to get a visa extension from the Foreigner's Registration Branch at the Police Commissioner's Office, who will make you pay a fine and may keep you waiting for weeks. So change your ticket and leave a day earlier."

"But if I change my ticket it's gonna cost me 100 euro!"

"What do you want? Pay another 100 euro, or get caught in the biggest bureaucratic nightmare you've had in your life?"

"Hmmmm..."

It's not often I try to help people with their travel arrangements. It's not a big thing on my 'to do' list, but when I see a friend heading into a messy conflict with Mumbai

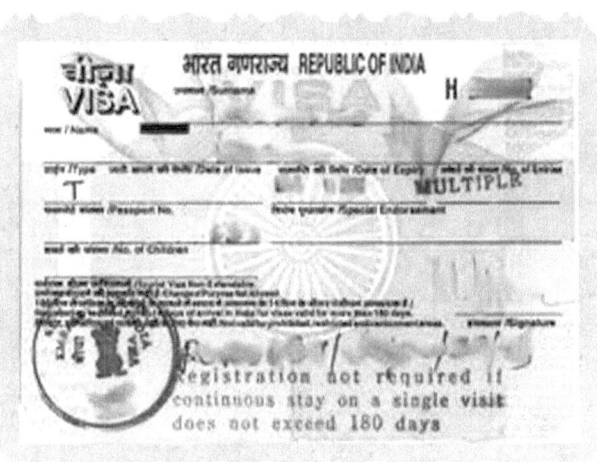

Airport's immigration control I have to say "Whoa! Are you sure you wanna go there?"

It wasn't always like this. In olden, golden days, immigration officials were more flexible creatures. I remember a story told by Mukta, Osho's gardener, who back in the early 70s overstayed her visa by several months.

Still blissed out from her time with Osho, she glided up to two airport immigration officers in Mumbai, dressed in her orange robe and mala, and presented her passport.

They looked at it.

"You've overstayed," they told her.

"Have I?"

"Yes, this is a serious matter. We can't let you go."

A beautiful, radiant smile lit up Mukta's face as she contemplated more time with Osho.

"Okay," she said, "I'll stay!"

They looked at each other, hurriedly stamped her passport and let her through.

As for Brits like myself, we didn't even need a visa.

With most Indians still looking nostalgically backwards at the glorious days of the Raj, we could come and go at our Imperial pleasure.

Not anymore. India has been traumatized by repeated terrorist attacks. Mumbai, especially, still shudders at the memory of the assault on the Taj Hotel in 2008. And one of the things that helps Indian authorities feel safer is to create lots and lots of regulations that are strictly enforced, especially concerning the movement of foreigners.

I remember, one time, approaching Mumbai airport's immigration control, hoping to leave on a Virgin Atlantic flight to London. My five-year visa was still valid, but foreigners staying more than 180 days in India are required to register with the local police and this I'd been unable to do. Pune police had stopped registering tourists.

What I should have done – which many sannyasins were doing at that time – was take a quick return flight to Sri Lanka before the 180 days were up, then re-enter India on the same five-year visa with a new stamp.

But I got lazy and figured "What the hell, it's only another two months... I'm leaving the country anyway... they'll probably waive me through..."

I was hoping immigration control would be crowded, with lines of people waiting, so I could slip through in the busy crush. But when I got there, for the first time in 38 years of leaving India, the place was absolutely empty. All the control booths were manned with immigration officials, but not a tourist in sight – just me. Bummer.

They got me. They stopped me. An offer to pay an on-the-spot 'fine' – the closest I dared come to uttering the word 'baksheesh' – was dismissed with a curt 'certainly not'. They sent me back to Pune where I struggled for 19 days to get exit clearance.

It was a nightmare. I got stuck with a power-tripping bureaucrat, while the man who could 'okay' my exit – unbeknown to me – was sitting in the next office. Eventually, I informed them all that I was a famous journalist from the UK who was going to write a story about the psychological torture of innocent tourists. I got the exit stamp within 24 hours – a miracle!

Never again. Now I happily apply for a six-month tourist visa, obey all the rules and keep my nose clean. No hassle, no problem.

When I'd finished telling this story to my friend, I looked at him and asked, "So, you still want to risk walking through immigration control after midnight?"

He smiled. "I'm going to the travel agent right now to change my ticket."

Pune Diary 42

The real thing

Normally, in life, when you want the real thing, you pay more for it. Naturally. It makes sense. Substitutes are cheaper and usually not as good.

In India, however, there is one item, in huge public demand, which makes this economic law stand on its head. If you want the real thing, you pay less. Much less.

To illustrate my point, allow me to take you on a short guided tour of Koregaon Park:

You are strolling along German Bakery Lane, enjoying the morning sunshine, and feel like having a cup of masala chai. On impulse, you walk to The 'O' Hotel, pass through the security check at the entrance and proceed to the diner on the ground floor, where you order your desired beverage.

It's not a bad drink, a bit like milky tea with a few spices, probably taken out of a packet in which everything was pre-mixed. For this refreshment, you find yourself paying Rs.155, or just less than two euro. By European standards, not a bad deal for a five-star hotel.

However, what you have just been drinking is not real masala chai; it is, at best, a very poor distant cousin.

Exiting The 'O' Hotel, you turn right on German Bakery Lane and within just a few metres find yourself standing at a street-side shack – nothing more than a table sitting under a small plastic roof by the side of the road.

On the table, a kerosene pump-action stove is blazing

away with a large aluminium kettle perched precariously
on top.

"Chai please."

Sanjay, the proprietor of this establishment, lifts the
kettle off the stove and pours a thick, hot, brown liquid
into a small plastic cup and gives it to you.

"How much?"

"Eight rupees."

Here we have the real deal: a genuine cup of masala chai
at a throwaway price.

This is the Indian working man's espresso: an intense
shot of sweet 'n spicy black tea that will kick start the day
and keep the body's motor running through the morning.

It's something everyone can afford and is sold on the
streets of every city, town and village throughout India.

Sanjay not only serves those who come to his stall.
He supplies all the shop owners and street vendors along

German Bakery Lane, with deliveries twice a day: once in the morning around 10:30 am and once in the afternoon around 4:30 pm.

He knows all about the Osho Resort. He worked there as a young man, while Osho was still alive, helping in the kitchen, the store room and other areas. He can recite an impressive list of all the sannyasin managers he worked with over the years.

I ask him for the recipe of his brew and he willingly shares it: black tea powder, milk, sugar, ginger and cardamom.

Ordinary folks like you and me can buy tea for making chai in any of Koregaon Park's general stores under the brand name 'Red Label'. It doesn't look like tea leaves – more like Nescafe, coming in the form of small dark-brown granules.

But, strictly speaking, this isn't the real thing. Street vendors like Sanjay make their chai with tea powder purchased at the Maharashtra Tea Store, just off MG Road, where, once upon a time, sannyasins used to go and change dollars for rupees at black market rates.

This tea sells for Rs.250 per kilo and is, as the name suggests, almost a powder... tiny little flakes that hardly look like tea at all. Yet this is the stuff that keeps India moving. This is the fuel that runs a nation.

Other chai rates in Koregaon Park vary from Rs.110 in Dario's to Rs.60 in Prems to Rs.55 in the Osho Resort. The Yogi Tree offers the most flexibility: a choice of Rs.30/50/80 depending on size.

Chai means 'tea' in Hindi and comes from the Chinese word 'chá', which, please note, is remarkably close to 'chan' the Chinese term for Zen. Both are efforts to keep awake.

Initiation: once, I was asked to make chai in the

Himalayas for a guru and his disciples. After sweating hard in the kitchen, I produced the brew and handed the guru a cup. He sipped. He paused. He looked at me and said, "You make good chai." YES!

Rebellion: once, in 1977, I attained brief but heroic status in the Pune ashram's kitchen by defying Deeksha, the all-powerful Italian momma, and making a big can of no-sugar chai. Against all her dire predictions – "is-a not-a wanted by-a sannyasins" – it was popular and sold out.

Communion: back in the 70s, on an endless train journey through Central India, while half asleep at 3:00 in the morning, after the train had stopped in the middle of nowhere at some empty, god-forsaken station, I heard a deep, mournful, ghostly cry approaching slowly along the platform:

"Chai... chai... chai wallah..."

The sound seemed timeless, eternal, other-worldly. In that moment, I felt I was listening to the very soul of India.

Time for a cuppa?

Pune Diary 43

The scent of a woman

The perfume hits me while I'm still 20 metres away from the bush. It's strong... so strong that it effectively interrupts my thoughts, which for any meditator must be an unexpected bonus. What I mean is: I cannot avoid noticing it. The scent envelopes me, demanding my full attention.

Osho once said, "Night Queen possess you, like a woman."

He knew what he was talking about, at least, as far as this flower and its fragrance is concerned. About the wider implications of his statement, I think I'd better not go there.

Called *Raat Raani* by locals here in Maharashtra, it's an evergreen, woody, ordinary-looking shrub that's known in English as Night Queen or, more scientifically, as Night-Blooming Cestrum.

During the day, I pass the bush without even noticing it, as it stands anonymously near the front gate of the house in which I'm living. And since the tiny flowers are sheathed in green cases it's not obvious during daylight hours that this innocuous-looking bush – standing not much taller than myself – is really a perfume bomb getting ready to explode.

It's only after dark that Night Queen announces the all-pervading potency of its presence. And it's only now, when the cold nights of the winter season have disappeared and given way to warm weather that the flowers really begin to bloom and release their fragrance.

When I leave the resort around 11:00 pm, walking along the back roads of Koregaon Park, engrossed in my thoughts, happy about the party I've just left, or anticipating the pleasure of sliding under my mosquito net, I suddenly find myself crossing the invisible boundary of Night Queen's zone of influence.

Its perfume captures my full and immediate attention. "You cannot ignore me," says Night Queen. "Stop. Stand still. Allow me to intoxicate you."

I yield to its demand and later, when I go to sleep, the scent of its perfume is still in my nostrils. If I was living at the front of the house, I'd have a hard time sleeping with such an intense fragrance hanging in the air. It may be a feminine, queen-like bush, but, like all men, I have times when I need to say, "Beloved, I need space."

I've always assumed that Night Queen is a deeply and

naturally Indian phenomenon, because it blends so well with the hot season and all the smells and fragrances of this country. Yet, so I'm told, it comes from the West Indies and was brought here only a century ago, whereupon it quickly naturalized itself and spread all over Southern Asia.

I guess, like me, it was just waiting for someone to import it into its spiritual home.

Other signs of the approaching hot season are here: dry leaves falling like rain on the streets of Koregaon Park; less air pollution now that the night watchmen aren't lighting fires to keep warm; dance meditations in Buddha Grove where the dancers seek out shadows cast by the trees, rather than standing in the sunshine.

As the heat increases, the *koyal*, or Indian cuckoo, gets noticeably louder and more active, with its rapid succession of cries: 'Whoop! Whoop! Whoop!' This morning, just before sunrise, a whole bunch of them were competing for my attention, along with train whistles, crows and the sound of the namaaz from a distant mosque.

As far as I was concerned the *koyals* won, because they were singing right outside my window.

Entomologists will note that the hot season also calls forth a bright pink beetle, stunningly day-glo in colour, which will insist on mating on road surfaces, with reckless disregard for traffic. There must be some who prefer mating in the bushes, or the species would be extinct.

Meanwhile, in the resort, Meera canteen has shut down and we all eat together in Zorba restaurant. Lots more people gather around the pool, but few actually swim – the water is still quite cool. Personally, I never put on my bathers here until April, when the temperature hits 38 or more, and this year that'll be too late. I'll be long gone...

Pune Diary 44

India's favourite cult

Crystal has big plans. He's renting motorbikes and setting up a tour.

"We start in Pune and head east to a town nobody's heard of," he tells me. "From then on, we're off the highway and on the back roads. No trucks. We head on down to Hampi, then to Goa, chill at the beach for a few days, then back here – two weeks, all inclusive."

He wants me to come. "I've been thinking of you," he confides. "What if we take you along and you teach us the Enneagram at the stops? You know, mix in a little meditation and awareness as part of the package."

It's a tempting offer, but comes a little late – at least for this trip. They're leaving in three days and I have a backlog of work for clients. Maybe next year.

Meanwhile, Crystal has lined up nine Royal Enfield motorbikes, mostly the classic Bullet 350cc model, but with a Thunderbird and other variations thrown in. He's got guys flying in from Germany to take part in the tour, plus a skilled mechanic who'll be riding with them.

Puffing on a beedi in the Plaza smoking temple, Crystal has come a long way since holding down a job as senior vice president in an investment corporation. He dropped out, discovered Osho, found himself a lovely girlfriend and has been riding Enfields for years. Now he wants to share his passion with others.

I understand his enthusiasm for this machine. It's really

the tour bike *par excellence* for India, with its wide, super-comfy seat, stable road holding capacity and reassuring 'doom...doom...doom' thumping sound of its engine as you cruise from town to town.

A few years back, I rode one of these monsters for 21 days through the Himalayas, with Ash and Deepesh, the *Riding High Tours* specialists.

Deepesh was a real cowboy. He could ride like the wind and once drove nonstop from Leh to Manali – usually a two or three day journey – just to take the sleeper bus to Delhi with a new girlfriend as she headed back to Holland. They'd met on the road in the mountains, leading Enfield tours in opposite directions. When they took their helmets off, it was love at first sight.

When I heard Deepesh was dead, I felt sure he'd flown off a mountain-side in Spiti Valley or Ladakh. Imagine my surprise when I learned he died from an asthma attack at his home in Brazil. I don't know if they buried his motorbike along with him, but they should have.

Royal Enfield was a British motorbike firm that began production in 1901 and then, in the 1950s, set up a subsidiary company in Madras (now Chennai), mainly to supply the Indian Army with a sturdy machine for patrolling the country's wild and endless borders.

The Army's first request was for 800 Bullets, a huge order at the time. Since Pune continues to be an army town – headquarters of Southern Command – you still see green-painted Enfields driven by soldiers, chugging around the town's Camp area.

In 1968, the parent company in England went out of business, but the subsidiary in Chennai thrived and gradually more and more people – Indians and tourists

alike – came to love the bike's power and style.

Now there are dozens of Enfield clubs throughout India and many tour operators regularly take visitors on extensive rides through all kinds of terrain. When I toured with Ash and Deepesh, we were riding mainly above 3000 metres and crossing passes at 5000 metres. The bikes were fine with everything they had to deal with, including ploughing through a freak snowstorm, fording rivers and passing army convoys on mountains.

I still remember, with a glow of pleasure, cruising with Ash and Deepesh into Leh, wearing my super-expensive Oakley goggles and acknowledging the admiring glances of ordinary tourists as we passed them in one long, throbbing line of motorbikes... the height of Enfield cool.

Royal Enfield is now the oldest motorcycle brand in the world still in production, with the Bullet model enjoying the longest motorcycle production run of all time. Success is due to the bike's 'cult' image, meaning that it's become 'the thing' to ride one as part of 'the Indian experience'. Exports to other countries are also booming.

Two weeks later, Crystal is back in Pune with a happy, suntanned crew of bikers, including several glamorous women who accompanied them. No accidents and no mechanical failures. He's all fired up for doing it again next winter. Maybe I'll go with him.

Not sure about the Enneagram mobile workshop, though. After all, how does a Seven ride an Enfield? Or a Four? Have to think about it...

Pune Diary 45

Tune of the thali

There is no menu in this restaurant. They don't ask you what you'd like to eat. You get what you're given and that's enough.

I like to get there about 12:50 pm, just before the rush.

It's a five minute stroll from the resort's back gate: walk to the end of Lane 2, risk life-threatening injuries by crossing North Main Road, enter Lane C, passing where the Ganesh temple used to be, ignore Buddha Paradise and steadily penetrate deeper and deeper into Rag Vilas... turn left, turn right... and there it is...

When you see it for the first time, you may think, "Hey, this isn't a restaurant, it's just a house!"

True enough. It's a house – with a living room converted into a restaurant.

The décor is functional. The seating Spartan. You sit on the floor on long red plastic cushions, or on plastic chairs outside in a covered corner of the yard.

In spite of my advancing years and stiffening limbs, I can still manage to squeeze into a space on the floor, sitting in a semi-lotus position.

Other customers include ageing hippies who somehow forgot to leave Pune, devotees of Dolano, students of various yoga schools and an occasional local businessman. But mainly the clientele consists of sannyasins like me.

Three or four large cooking pots stand in a row on a side table. Their contents are freshly cooked, waiting for the lunchtime crowd.

Almost immediately, after sitting down, a round silver plate is set in front of me, which invariably contains: a silver bowl of dal, a smaller bowl of beans or some special kind of veg, and a bigger mix of sabji – cooked mixed vegetables – served on the plate itself.

Indians take rice later, but Westerners like it with the main course, so my plate has a generous dollop of white rice as well.

Rotis come flying off the stove, where they are toasted over a naked flame, arriving all hot and puffy. There's no space here for a roti oven, but the gas ring on the stove does a fair job of making this round-style traditional bread.

You can eat as much as you like. Personally, I never get beyond two helpings of everything, but, theoretically at least, you can go on... and on...

Overseeing the process are Nitin and Gita. They opened their restaurant about eight years ago, naming it 'Raga' – the Hindi word for 'tune' or 'melody' – and have been doing a fair trade ever since.

They have one offering: thali, a simple, standard meal that's a central pillar of India's cultural cuisine. When they started, Nitin and Gita charged 40 rupees per thali - extra, of course, for lassi, curd and chai - but now their price is 80 rupees, reflecting the increase in basic food costs over the years.

There are at least three more places offering thali in the surrounding area. All of them are okay and all about the same price, but I find them either too oily or too spicy for my taste. Raga's plain and wholesome style hits the spot, for me and many others.

The word 'thali' is Hindi for 'plate', but it's come to mean a special combo of rice, dal, roti and sabji, plus a few optional extras like curd and pickle. Here at Raga, it's pretty basic but in a fancy restaurant the number of bowls per plate increases dramatically.

For a five-star thali, there used to be nothing better than Mayur, up on East Street, close to MG Road, but, alas, the place has shut down. Mayur's thali had at least five or six bowls of veg, plus dal and curd, and a dazzling range of desserts, including shrikhand – my all-time favourite.

In 1977, Haridas, one of Osho's longtime sannyasins, invited me for my first-ever thali to the Dreamland Hotel, near Pune railway station, where they offered Gujarati-style food, plus dessert on Sundays. Thereafter, we went every Sunday lunchtime.

Thali every day would be boring, so I have a few non-thali options in Koregaon Park, including *Yummy*

Yummy Potatoes – boiled potatoes drowned in an amazing tomatoey-creamy-herby sauce – offered at the Yogi Tree and a generous plateful of avocado salad at Dario's.

Mostly, though, being a lazy guy, I eat in the resort. But it's nice to know that, just along the back street, Nitin and Gita's tuneful thalis are available any time I want.

By the way, Nitin also makes a fair lassi, whipping it up as you watch… sweet, plain, or with fruit. If I take that, too, then it becomes a sizeable meal and a stroll back to the resort is definitely needed to walk it off.

What's that you say? Stop off at the Plaza café for cappuccino and brownies? Sure, why not…

Pune Diary 46

Kings of the backstreets

He sits in the middle of the road, where two streets meet, expecting all the cars, motorbikes and bicycles to go around him. The strange thing is, they do! Indians have long been accustomed to the traffic hazard of local stray dogs sitting and lying in the road and usually give way to them.

Of course, this doesn't happen on busy streets like North Main Road, but on the quieter side streets it's a regular feature of urban life.

Every lane of Koregaon Park has its small pack of stray dogs, owned by nobody and living on hand-outs from compassionate locals, or, more reliably, from food garbage cast aside by restaurants and street food stalls.

However, the white dog that I'm passing by on Lane Two this morning isn't your standard 'kutta' - the Hindi term for a street dog. He looks more like a cross-breed between a kutta and a house dog, which happens from time to time.

A normal kutta has the classic brown colouring and short hair of the original landrace dogs that have been living side-by-side with human beings in this part of the world for thousands of years.

Officially called the Indian Pariah Dog, or 'Indog', this is one of the oldest species in the world and has never been bred. It's evolved through natural selection and has been studied scientifically, for example in National Geographic's 'Search for the Original Dog'.

It was the English who started calling these dogs

'pariah', sometime in the 19th century. It began in the city of Madras, where drummers from low caste communities were referred to in the Tamil language as 'pariahs'.

Gradually, this term was extended to include all low-caste servants, then it mutated to become a condemnatory name for social outcasts, then was extended to include stray dogs.

So, that's how these dogs got a bad name for themselves.

Generally speaking, they are not aggressive. I pass by them every day, when walking to the resort from my home, and they never give me any trouble. They've learned, over the centuries, that if they want to get along with mankind they need to keep a low profile.

In the slums, they get adopted by families and become good guard dogs, suspicious of strangers and friendly and protective with children.

One interesting character trait: being highly intelligent, they easily get bored and refuse to play repetitive games like 'fetch stick', which some domesticated breeds will do for hours. I like that. In my eyes, it gives pariah dogs a certain dignity.

It's not all plain sailing, though. In a city of more than 5 million people like Pune, there are an estimated 40,000 stray dogs, with inevitable clashes between dogs and humans that result in about 35 bites per day.

Rabies is endemic in the dog population, so a bite can be serious. A couple of years ago, a rogue dog entered Koregaon Park on Lane 6 and bit 14 people in a single day. One person died from rabies and the rest had to take medication against it.

Usually, though, these dogs are far more interested in other dogs than humans. Fat, overweight house dogs being taken for walks on a leash make them particularly excited and provoke much barking, teeth baring and snarling.

For me, the biggest danger is that some of these dogs are really cute, some have genuine dignity and grace, and then it's hard not to feed and pet them. But if I do, I'll have a friend for life, waiting for me every morning as I leave my house, so I resist the temptation and just admire them from a distance.

Some are miserable and pathetic. One dog, obviously abandoned by its owner, tried every day to follow me – or anyone else who was passing – in the hope of finding a new home.

It never did. But I was heartened, coming back a year later, to see it had adjusted to street life and was no longer whimpering and whining as before.

One incident I vividly remember: walking along a dark street, late one night, I suddenly heard a low growl close behind me.

My body's reaction was instantaneous: a shock of electricity up my spine, a dramatic increase in my heart rate and a knot of fear in my stomach. I'm bald, so my hair didn't stand on end, but if it could have, it would have.

It was amazing: thousands of years of civilization disappeared in an instant. As far as my body was concerned I was again in the jungle, facing life-threatening danger from behind: all systems alert... fight or flight.

Intelligence prevailed: "There are no tigers in Pune," I told myself, "So it must be a dog."

I stopped, slowly turned around and made the classic gesture of reaching down to the road surface to pick up a rock. The rock wasn't there, but the dog got the message. He ran.

Pune Diary 47

From light to darkness

Birth is thus
Death is thus
Verse or no verse
What is the fuss?

With this little poem, composed just before his death, we leave Ta Hui, the intellectual Zen Master. The Evening Meeting is over. In our white robes, we move slowly out of Osho Auditorium to the shoe racks, slip on our flip-flops, then shuffle quietly towards the exit, carrying our black discourse chairs with us.

As we emerge from the building, a nearly-full moon shines down brilliantly upon us and I have to stop to drink in the scene. I'm standing at the top of the stone stairs, resting my arms on the parapet, watching as two streams of white robes pass down the steps on either side of me, joining at the bottom and flowing in a single river across the walkway, between the lakes.

All these white robes are kinda glowing in the dark, as if illuminated by ultraviolet light, but, as people reach the other side, they disappear among the trees, vanishing into darkness. The scene is surreal, from a movie about Atlantis or some lost civilization.

I can forget, for a moment, that I'm surrounded by the chaos and madness of India's eighth biggest city, growing at the mind-boggling rate of a million people every decade.

On a night like this, it's tempting to stay outside, enjoying the moonlight. But I have other plans. After dinner, I meet in the Plaza with 20-30 people and we are led silently around the front of Krishna House and down into Chaitanya Chambers.

Memories cling to the walls here, calling to me as I descend the stairs. Here, I did Encounter with Teertha and Turiya. Here, I did Primal with Naresh, Geetesh and Purna. Here, I came face-to-face with fear and lived to tell the tale.

One memory makes me smile. My parents visited the ashram in '79 and my father, sitting in Vrindavan Canteen, listening each day to the cries and screams coming from underneath us, jokingly rechristened the underground group rooms 'the chambers of correction'.

Actually, he got it wrong. We were learning how to be incorrect. But that's another story.

Down here, in the chambers, claustrophobia is part of the

package. I've been told there's an escape hatch somewhere, in case fire blocks the exit, but I've never seen it.

We walk along the narrow, underground corridor to the end room, leave our shoes in the racks and step inside. The atmosphere is casual and relaxed. We wear street clothes and can take bags in with us.

The floor is covered with black mattresses and we sit comfortably on black meditation chairs with black pillows for back support. Black, you will note, is the dominant colour. And it's about to get a whole lot blacker.

The lights are slowly turned down and everything vanishes into darkness. The last light to be extinguished is an illuminated crystal. As it disappears, the room disappears, the people disappear... the world disappears.

This has to be the simplest meditation ever invented. You just sit, with your eyes open, looking into darkness. For a while, you go on staring out into nothing, because that's our habit – that's the way our energy usually goes, pouring out of our eyes as we continuously look at the world around us.

But slowly, the brain takes account of this new and unusual situation, and tells the eyes, "Hey guys, there's really nothing to look at, so you can relax."

Just to make sure, I look around the room – or, rather, where the room ought to be. It's weird. It was here a moment ago. I was surrounded by people, sitting very close to me. I look in their direction, trying to see shapes and outlines in the darkness. Nothing. Nada. My environment is, as it's supposed to be, totally black.

After a while, an energetic shift happens. Energy stops flowing out of the eyes and instead the darkness starts to flow in. It begins to feel like the darkness is inside me.

I remember Osho saying something about this: receive the darkness inside and take it home with you after the meditation. An interesting idea. It seems to happen by itself, anyway, without any decision on my part.

After 45 minutes, a gong announces the second and final stage of the meditation: lie down and feel as if the darkness is a womb. It's nice to lie down, but hard to keep my eyes open. When my eyelids do close, I notice there's no difference: open or closed, it's the same darkness.

A final gong, the meditation is over and light returns to the room. Slowly, we get up, file out of the room, along the corridor, up the stairs and into the open. Yes, the world is still here, where we left it an hour ago.

I head for the Plaza. It's an evening of romantic songs and Multiversity Plaza has been turned into a giant pink-lace boudoir. But I'm not staying, or looking for a partner. I already have a companion.

I'm going home with the darkness inside me.

Pune Diary 48

Samsara maya hai

It all happened so fast. I was sitting in the smoking temple, even though I don't smoke, when this attractive young woman throws herself in my lap and demands a photo – even though we don't take photos in the resort.

Naturally, I have to laugh, so it looks like we're having a great time, even though we hardly know each other. Next thing I know, she's uploading the photo – using her mobile, not even moving from my lap – and posting it on Facebook.

So, in seconds, the message goes out across the world that I'm one hot hombre at the ripe old age of 68, even though I haven't made love in almost a year. In India, they have an ancient saying: *Samsara maya hai...* the world is an illusion.

Maybe it's not the world that's an illusion. Maybe it's just Facebook. Anyway, the fact is, life continues to surprise me, which I guess is the way it should be.

Until recently, in the absence of any instinctive urges, I was getting used to the idea that my sexual 'machinery' – as Osho calls it in his jokes – had retired from active duty and was moving into a permanent state of *brahmacharya*.

My body didn't mind. My energy didn't mind. "Ah yes," they said. "Time to ease up on the testosterone, old chap. Relax. Kick back. Enjoy not being driven by your hormones."

My mind did mind, but since sex is supposed to disappear

around 42, I figured I'd already added an extra 26 years, so maybe it was time to act my age.

Shortly thereafter, however, I happened to meet an attractive visitor from Europe, about 50 years old, who told me she was suffering from tension in her head and shoulders.

"I know the feeling," I said, sympathetically, as a chronic laptop user.

"Massage is too invasive," she sighed.

"I'll give you a cranio session," I offered.

This was odd, since I have zero training in cranio. But experts have told me that 50 percent of cranio's effect comes from sitting silently, with presence, meditating with the client. So I looked up a few cranio hand positions on YouTube and... hey, guess what? It worked.

"My neck feels much better," she told me, as we had tea on my balcony afterwards.

Of course, this was a thinly-disguised 'let's-get-to-know-each-other' strategy, but I was lazy and didn't pursue it. So I was pleasantly surprised, a few days later, when my new friend said, "I'd like you to invite me to tea again."

That afternoon, on my balcony, I commented, "You know, when an attractive woman invites herself to tea, there's usually something more on going on. Is it true?"

She blushed and whispered "Yes."

So that's how my ten-month romance with celibacy came to an end. Of course, we both know this is an 'in-the-moment' affair. I'm leaving India in a week and she's staying another five months. Such is the nature of meetings in Pune.

Samsara maya hai... The world may not be an illusion, but, like the sages say, its pleasures are fleeting.

Meanwhile, the young woman who jumped in my lap in the smoking temple is begging me to give her a guided tour of the resort. An unusual role for me, but why not?

We begin with Lao Tzu House and I soon realize she knows nothing. Well, of course, why would she? She only just arrived. She knows how to do Dynamic Meditation and that's about it.

Funny, she's been given a room on the roof of Lao Tzu House – something I would've died for, decades ago – and she has no idea what's below her bed. Back in the fabled days of 'Poona One' this was the holiest of holies. This was the house where Osho lived. And even now, it has special status in the hearts of sannyasins, because this is where Osho's ashes are kept, in a marble tomb, in the Samadhi.

"The... what?" she asks, puzzled.

"Oh, sorry, I mean Chuang Tzu Auditorium," I reply.

"You mean, the big black building, where we do Dynamic?"

"Er, no, that's Osho Auditorium. Come with me."

We walk down memory lane together, passing where the old Lao Tzu gate and guard hut used to be, along the side of the house, around by the Rolls Royce and into Osho's garden.

Here, the 'No Entry' sign has been removed, so I feel free to show her Osho's dining room, his bedroom, and then we tiptoe through the plants - "watch out for snakes" - and peer through the tinted glass into Chuang Tzu Auditorium. At this late hour in the afternoon, I know it's empty.

"Up there..." I point to Lao Tzu's upstairs group room. "That was an open balcony. Osho gave his first discourses there, in 1974, before this auditorium was built..."

It's enjoyable, giving this tour, but a little surreal. I'm standing here, in this silent garden, with a charming young woman, on a sunny afternoon, telling stories about things that happened 40 years ago, before she was born.

Did they really happen? And, if she can meditate without knowing any of this, does any of it really matter?

Samsara maya hai...

Life moves swiftly. Memories fade. *It all happened so fast.*

Someday, not so far away, two people will be sitting in the Plaza smoking temple and one will ask the other, "You remember the guy who wrote that Pune diary... what was his name?"

Pune Diary 49

This house is not for sale

In any normal neighbourhood, when people want to sell their houses, they put up a 'For Sale' sign. You don't expect people who don't want to sell their houses to put up signs saying 'Not For Sale'.

But Koregaon Park is no ordinary neighbourhood. It contains some of the most expensive real estate in India. Every wealthy industrialist and businessman wants to make a home here – and they're willing to plunk down lots of cash for the privilege.

You never see a 'For Sale' sign. The deals are negotiated, the contracts signed and sealed before anyone knows what's happened.

Lane 3 tells the story. Until recently, there was a big house at No.73. It wasn't particularly old and it wasn't particularly beautiful. But it was a big solid bungalow and looked good for another hundred years.

Now there's just a big hole in the ground – a very big hole. So big, one wonders if the new owner is going to build a bungalow, as Koregaon Park's regulations allow, or whether this is going to be the first rule-breaking apartment complex to get inside the park.

Next door, is No.74, once inhabited by Folli, an impeccably dressed Indian gentleman and long-time friend of the Osho Resort. He drove a vintage car, spoke old-fashioned, upper class English, hosted dinner parties for sannyasins and even rented out some of his rooms for workshops and groups.

Folli now lives in Mumbai, but his house remains the same, just repainted white by its new owners.

The next property, No. 75, is styled in the manner of an Italian villa. Recently, it disappeared behind newly-built, high walls - a sure sign that it is occupied, protected and definitely not on the market.

It is at No.76 that we find a large sign announcing 'This Property Belongs to Ms. Lia Dubash and is Not For Sale'. Clearly, Ms. Dubash is fed up with being harassed by hungry property speculators and wannabe Koregaon Park residents and wants it known, once and for all, that she is not selling up.

It's easy to see why people think the property might be available. It looks like all the bungalows did, 30 or 40 years ago, before the real estate gold rush began. The walls are low, crumbling and badly maintained. The wrought iron gate is sagging on its hinges. The driveway is full of weeds. The house itself is half hidden behind untrimmed trees and bushes.

I really don't think anything has been done to this house since I first saw it in 1976. It's a miracle it's still standing. But Ms. Dubash, whoever she is and wherever she may be - in Dubai, Mumbai, or Los Angeles - isn't willing to give it up, even though it's probably worth a cool US $5 million.

Maybe she's planning to retire here one day. Maybe she grew up here and keeps it for sentimental reasons. One thing's for sure, sitting on this plot of gold and not selling, Ms. Dubash isn't short of a few pennies.

Meanwhile, those frustrated Puneites, eagerly climbing the social ladder and desperate to be as close as possible to the park, have another option.

On North Main Road, just outside the boundary of the

original four lanes of Koregaon Park, two massive towers are heading skywards, their billboards offering luxury apartments with flowery phrases:

'Aria: the Status Icon, with Exclusive Sky Villas'.

'Windermere: A Private Community of Uber-Luxurious, Ultra-Exclusive Apartments'.

No less than 12 storeys of apartments rise out of these construction sites. For a mere US $400,000, you can look down from your new apartment upon the Koregaon Park mansions that are so coveted.

For years, I lived at No.121, a spacious mansion on Lane No.4, where Vijay, the Maharani of Morvi, rented out a dozen-or-so rooms to sannyasins. Now, standing in her back yard, I crane my neck and look upward at the monster that has risen just beyond her retaining wall.

I used to stand here and look across open fields to Mogul

Gardens. I used to think Mogul Gardens was big, but its three or four levels seem like villas for pygmies, compared to this giant.

All common sense says it's crazy to build more apartment blocks on North Main Road, which is already choked with traffic. But such is the demand for housing in this part of town that no one is willing to stop the boom.

Meanwhile, as we drive along Lane No.3, Shiva, my rickshaw wallah, recalls that at the age of nine he bicycled every day to No.70 to deliver a lunch tiffin to a sannyasin who lived in the old mansion.

Now, in its place, rises Poonawalla Mansion, complete with Greco-Roman columns and a Michelangelo-style dome, a massive statement of wealth by Cyrus S. Poonawalla, India's 14th richest citizen and chairman of the Pune Turf Club.

In Koregaon Park, there's only one property that defeats Poonawalla... and, oh yes, I'm going there for the Evening Meeting... "Back gate, please Shiva!"

Pune Diary 50

Time to go...

I like the synchronicity. It feels right that my last Pune diary in this series should be about a death celebration. It's time to leave, to say goodbye.

The man who gives us the celebration is Swami Anand Manoharbharti, an elderly Indian sannyasin whose face seems familiar to me, although I didn't know him personally.

A small podium, covered with purple cloth and scattered with rose petals and flowers, is created in Osho Auditorium. A live band kicks in and about 100 people are dancing and singing as the body is brought in on a bamboo stretcher, carried by half a dozen men.

I stand close to the body as it is gently lowered onto the podium. I feel the need to look death in the face, because somewhere, deep inside, I just don't get it.

Even though my intellect tells me, rationally, logically, one day I'm going to die, it doesn't really penetrate. How do I know? Because, if it did, all of my trivial worries, concerns and day-to-day mindfucks would evaporate like smoke before a hurricane.

We sing, we scatter rose petals on the body and after a few minutes the stretcher is lifted and carried out, on its way to the burning ghats.

But there's a new twist to this familiar routine. At the bottom of the auditorium stairs, a rather handsome trolley, or cart, is waiting. Basically, it's an upmarket version of those multipurpose, wooden carts on bicycle wheels that are pushed around the streets of every Indian city, piled with bananas, vegetables, scrap metal or anything else that can be bought or sold.

This one, however, cost Rs.60,000 to make, complete with hydraulic suspension. That's why it looks so elegant.

"These bodies are heavy and some of the guys who carry the stretchers are getting old," explained one resort official, a veteran organiser of many death celebrations.

So the body is gently lowered onto the cart, then joins a group of drummers who strike up an infectious rhythm and soon the whole procession is moving off towards the ghats.

Once we're out of the gate and on the street, the music, clapping and dancing really get going. Here's one moment when we can all be as loud as we like, without bothering about the neighbours. In the face of death, all objections cease.

Ahead of the crowd, colourful fireworks shoot jets of smoke, sparks and tiny balls of glowing light into the air. All the traffic on Lane No.1 has to stop. Everything stops for death – that's just the way it is.

I'm wondering what will happen when we hit North Main Road, but I needn't worry. A couple of courageous, uniformed security guards from the resort stride out onto the road, blowing whistles and waving their arms. They look like cops, so all the cars stop.

The procession dances its way down German Bakery Lane, along the narrow street at the bottom and down to the ghats by the river.

Some well-meaning authority has spent a lot of money making the ghats look nice, freshly painted, with new

roofs and good lighting. Pity, I liked it funky, the way it was before. The old India is disappearing and I cling to its memory in vain.

In one of the pits, the body is lowered onto a bed of wood and dried cow dung patties. The drummers keep up a lively beat and more wood is piled on top until the body disappears.

There is silence, as the musicians take a well-earned break. Someone taps me on the shoulder from behind.

"Do you want to sing?" a voice whispers. Someone remembers that, in the past, I was always singing with the drummers at the ghats.

"Only if you do," I reply, so we count to three and launch into the theme song of every sannyasin burning that ever happened here:

"Walk into the holy fire... step into the holy flame..."

Soon the whole crowd is singing with us.

The drummers support us, softly at first, then, as we start clapping and speeding up the song, the beat gradually gets louder until – just in time, because we can't sing this loudly for much longer – they take over again.

The funeral pyre is lit by relatives of the departing soul and soon it's blazing fiercely, with flames shooting up towards the roof.

I've heard Osho say that one of the reasons why Hindus burn the body is to provide concrete evidence to the person who just died that he is, in fact, dead.

I guess it's like this: the consciousness looks down upon the scene, sees the body disappearing in flames, and realises, "Holy shit, that's me! I must be dead!"

It helps with the transition into the unknown, so they say.

The fire will burn for hours, but after another half-hour the drummers finish their gig with three shouts of 'Osho!' People start to leave, including me. I make my way home to take a shower and wash my clothes – as advised after being close to a burning body – and then return to the resort for a welcome cup of chai.

Tomorrow, I start packing. The day after that, I take a taxi to Mumbai and fly to Europe.

I notice that my mind is fondly assuming I'll be back next winter; that the resort will still be here, that everything will continue according to the lifestyle I've been following for years now.

But none of it is certain.

Life, as Osho once told me, is under no obligation to fulfil my expectations.

What is real, right now, is 'goodbye'.

So, goodbye Pune... and thank you.

Epilogue – 1

What was he like?

As we speed through the second decade of the 21st century, people still ask me "What was it like to be with Osho? What was he like as a person? How did it feel to meet him face to face?"

Let me put it this way: on those occasions when I sat in front of him in darshan, for those moments, it felt like I was the most important person in the world, or the only person in the world, or both. This wasn't just my experience. It was everybody's experience.

It was the result of sitting in front of a human being who is giving you his total attention, a man who is one hundred percent present, here and now.

When he looked at you, smiled and gently asked, "How about you?" everything else disappeared. It was just you and him. The entire population of the world and, indeed, the universe itself, had just become completely irrelevant and probably non-existent.

Not only that, I had the feeling – and again, this was something many people commented on – that he saw me as a buddha. He had the capacity, the love and compassion, to look past all the bullshit of the personality and see my essential being.

Small wonder, then, that we floated out of such meetings on a white puffy cloud of bliss, gliding along the footpaths of the ashram, our feet barely touching the ground. It usually took a couple of hours to come down.

As you can imagine, these kinds of experiences caused problems at the office.

Dreamy-eyed women would wander into Krishna House, sit down in front of Laxmi, Osho's personal secretary, and announce "Bhagwan wants me to move into the ashram" (in those days, back in the 70s, he was called 'Bhagwan Shree Rajneesh').

Then Laxmi would have to patiently explain that the ashram's accommodation programme wasn't run via messages received through divine communion, mystical dreams, or on the astral plane. Any changes Osho wanted to make would be transmitted verbally to her during their daily meeting.

It wasn't only the women. On one occasion, after darshan, I became convinced that if I could slip a note to Osho's personal caretaker, Vivek, instead of going through the bureaucratic channels of the office, he would be sure to offer me a room – I was living outside at the time.

Of course, Vivek gave the note to Laxmi and I was told to grow up and act my age.

Poor Laxmi! The things she had to deal with.

But, really, it was amazing the place functioned at all, because all kinds of esoteric experiences were happening to many people, including me.

One time, I was lying in my bed, under my mosquito net, on a warm silent Indian night, when a sudden breeze blew in through the window. It was Osho, as if carried on the wind – or maybe he was the wind.

I didn't see him. I felt him, with total certainty and clarity, in all his freshness and friendliness. He didn't have anything to say. He was just checking up on me, giving me a loving 'hello' and then departing as mysteriously as he came.

Another time, during darshan, I was lying down at the back, not really participating, while Osho was doing some kind of energy event at the front with another sannyasin.

Suddenly, without warning and without any effort or intention on my part, I popped up, out of my body, and was floating about a metre above it.

It was like escaping from a high security prison. I had the sensation that I'd been contained not only by my physical body but by several layers of subtle energy bodies, all of which had now opened.

I barely had time to realise what was happening when "Whump!" I was back inside, with all doors closed. It was then that I realised how powerfully we are bound to the body.

On another occasion, when I was living inside the ashram, I'd skipped the early morning Dynamic Meditation and was lying sleepily in my bed when a massive roar erupted in the distance – from Buddha Hall – as the meditation entered its cathartic stage and everyone started screaming and shouting.

Somehow, the energy of that sound rolled like a wave through the ashram, into my room, into my feet and up through my body, pushing me gently out of the top of my head.

"Ooh, I'm out!" I exclaimed myself, in a kind of nowhere land. But then I panicked. What if I couldn't return to my body?

"My legs!" I shouted and kicked them hard. In a second, I was back inside and immediately regretting my cowardice.

"You fool! Couldn't you have stayed out a bit longer, so we could've had time to look around?" I scolded myself. It might have been fun, walking through walls, poking my nose into other people's rooms.

But it was too late. The opportunity had passed. Time to get up, take my physical body for a shower and then to breakfast. This was the real challenge of being in Pune in those days: to accept all these strange goings on and still lead a relatively 'normal' life.

Excerpt from Anand Subhuti's book about his life with Osho, titled 'My Dance with a Madman'.

Epilogue – 2

Looking out, Looking in

"Self-indulgence to the point of madness."

That was how one indignant British journalist described our lifestyle with Osho.

A former newspaper reporter myself, I could see his point. Journalists try to make sure the public maintains a high level of interest in the world surrounding us. This includes the 'serious issues' of our time – economic problems, political crises, unemployment, poverty, famine, conflict, war – and trivial stuff like fashion, sport, gossip, scandal and entertainment.

How can one simply turn one's back on it all and look within?

Well, actually, for me it was easy.

By the time I went to India, I'd already studied the sayings of several spiritual mystics and one of Gautam the Buddha's statements stuck with me:

We are what we think. With our thoughts we make the world.

In other words, the state of the world is our own creation. Not the natural world of rivers, mountains and deserts, but the social world of human beings.

We are continuously thinking it into existence, because this is the way we want it. For example, there is no such thing as 'the United Kingdom'. It's just an idea. It's nothing more than a thought, sustained by several million people. A piece of coloured cloth becomes a 'national flag' and an ordinary old woman is transformed into a 'queen' just because we happen to think so.

The media's job is to support the kind of reality we want to see, by continuously reflecting our thoughts back to us. Gossip about the Royal Family, votes in the House of Commons, championship football games, TV talent contests, celebrity interviews... it all feeds and sustains our social paradigm.

Content isn't important. It's the process that matters, because that's what keeps us looking outside instead of inside. As the Canadian philosopher Marshall McLuhan once famously said, "The medium is the message."

And the medium's message is: "Believe in this world we create together."

So, having understood my role in maintaining the collective illusion, I decided to explore my personal reality instead. That's why I quit. And when I arrived in Pune, in 1976, and Osho began one of his discourses with the words "Only individuals exist – society is an illusion," I knew I'd found a mystic who was speaking my language.

Excerpt from Anand Subhuti's book about his life with Osho, titled 'My Dance with a Madman'.

.